Passion
for
Jesus

Passion for Jesus

MIKE BICKLE

CREATION
HOUSE
BOOKS ABOUT SPIRIT-LED LIVING
ORLANDO, FLORIDA

Creation House
Strang Communications Company
600 Rinehart Road
Lake Mary, FL 32746
Web site: http://www.creationhouse.com

First printing, November 1993
Second printing, April 1994
Third printing, June 1994
Fourth printing, September 1994
Fifth printing, March 1995
Sixth printing, July 1995
Seventh printing, November 1995
Eighth printing, March 1996
Ninth printing, September 1996
Tenth printing, March 1997
Eleventh printing, August 1997

*I dedicate this book first to the many faithful
members of Metro Vineyard Fellowship of
Kansas City, whose passion for Jesus has
strengthened my heart over the last eleven years.
Their friendship has refreshed me often
and has really made the difference in my life.
What a privilege and joy to serve such willing
and dedicated people whose hearts pant hard
after God. They are people who have refused
to let me camp in the comfort zone.
They have continually encouraged me
to lead them forward in obedience to follow
the Lamb wherever He leads. They have faithfully
stood strong with me through times of blessing
and adversity. I love them for having
such loving courage and loyal friendship.*

*Second, I want to express my deepest
appreciation and gratitude to John Wimber
and the association of Vineyard churches.
They have provided a safe place
for our church family.
Their love and leadership have made
a significant impact upon us.
I deeply appreciate their loving embrace.
My debt to John Wimber's tender fathering
leadership is immense. May God raise up
a thousand spiritual fathers like him
whose humility and passion for Jesus
provide the context for many to grow
mighty in the grace of God.*

ACKNOWLEDGMENTS

First, I want to express my deepest appreciation to Jane Joseph and Susan Van Leeuwen for their many hours of laborious toil at the computer. Blessed are these bond servants of Jesus who will surely be called great in the Lord's kingdom.

Also, much thanks to Judy Doyle and Walter Walker, whose invaluable writing skills and profound insights have significantly molded this book. What a delight to work with such gifted yet humble people.

Last but not least, to Stephen Strang, who first envisioned a book that would focus on inspiring in people's hearts a holy passion for Jesus. I'm thankful for the sweet times of fellowship with him around this subject that resulted in the direction to write this book.

CONTENTS

Jesus said that the greatest commandment is to love God with all of our hearts, souls and minds (Matt. 22:37). Actually doing this commandment is the key to all of life. When the church loves God, it releases the power of God on earth. The church will never "love one another" nor the world until it first loves God. In light of this I am continually amazed at how little attention the church gives to this greatest of all commandments.

Christians demonstrate a consistent tendency to put almost any good thing ahead of loving God. Some of us make Bible study more important than loving God. Some of us pursue doctrinal purity more than we pursue the man Christ Jesus. Others of us put various forms of ministry like evangelism or caring for the poor ahead of the Lord Jesus. In some cases these good things even become a substitute for God.

Please don't misunderstand me. All of these things should be done. I don't believe that we can love the Bible or ministries too much. Rather we can love God too little in comparison with these things.

In my opinion, the greatest danger facing the church today does not come from without the church, but from within. It is not the New Age nor secular humanism that is crippling the effectiveness of the church today. It is the lack of love for God, the lukewarmness of the church, that is its greatest enemy today. A lukewarm, loveless version of Christianity may succeed in propagating a little religion here and there, but it will never capture the heart of a dying world.

What does it mean to love God with all of our hearts, souls and minds? Some have tried to define loving God as obeying God. Obedience is surely part of loving God, but we all know that you can obey someone without really loving that person. Love is not only obedience, but it is also passion. Obedience without passion for God is not love; it is only discipline. And if discipline is all we have, in the end discipline will fail us. But a man in love, a woman in love, will never give up (Song 8:6-7).

Passion for Jesus will conquer a thousand sins in our lives. But how do we get passion, and how do we cultivate it? Why and how do serious Christians lose their passion for God? How do they find it again? All of these questions and many more are addressed in this book not only with skill, but also with a refreshing honesty.

Mike Bickle's book, *Passion for Jesus*, is filled with wonderful insights into the greatest of all commandments. These insights were not derived from an academic study of Scripture, but rather from the pursuit of a person. Mike has spent his adult life attempting, above all else, to acquire a consuming passion for the Son of God.

Anyone who knows Mike Bickle, knows that insofar as he is consciously able, he has subordinated everything in his life to this one goal: acquiring and promulgating passion for the glorious person who sits at the right hand of the Father in heaven. And therein lies the power of this book.

Jack Deere, Th.D.
Author and lecturer
Fort Worth, Texas
October 1993

An Affectionate God

No one can come face-to-face with what God is like and ever be the same. Seeing His true image touches the depths of our temperament, bringing us to spiritual wholeness and maturity. Beholding the glory of who He is and what He has done renews our minds, strengthens us and transforms us.

In John 8:32 Jesus tells us that we will know the truth, and the truth will set us free. We long to be free — emotionally and spiritually. Yet Jesus says that freedom comes with knowing the truth. And we must start where Jesus says to start.

Since knowing the truth sets us free, then what we know

has a great impact on our emotional makeup. Thus, the way to our emotions is through our minds.

What truths must we know to be free?

First and most important, who is God? What is He like? What kind of personality does He have? Our ideas about God — who He is and what He is like — come naturally through our relationships with earthly authority figures. When these are distorted, so are our ideas about God.

I believe the greatest problem in the church is that we have an entirely inadequate and distorted idea of God's heart. We can experience short-term renewal through prayer and ministry. But to achieve long-term renewal and freedom we must change our ideas about who God is.

In your most private thoughts, what do you believe God's personality is like? Your entire spiritual future is related to how you answer this question in the secret place of your heart, because inaccurate ideas of God will have a negative emotional impact on us.

For instance, if you are a sincere believer and you stumble in sexual sin, your heart is broken, and you cry out to God. But how does He feel about you right then?

The second truth we must know to be free is, who are we in God?

Both of these truths are vital to our living full and complete lives. But here I want to focus on who God is.

God will satisfy our hungry hearts when He reveals Himself to us. As we encounter the awesome holiness and power of His personality we will have the power to overcome temptation.

God Himself will heal our emotional wounds, removing the scars. He ignites us to holy, passionate affection for a deeper understanding of the divine excellencies, perfections and passions of our Lord Jesus Christ.

A revelation of the true knowledge of our King will renew the body of Christ from the inside out. There are four key elements of the gospel that will lead believers to that revelation.

1. Who God is

2. What He has done

3. What we can receive

4. What we should do

The church places most of its emphasis on the last three: what God has done for us in Christ; the forgiveness and inheritance we receive as adopted children; and what we should do to receive and walk in them. We need to continue preaching these things faithfully. But the foundational element — who God is — is tragically absent in many of our messages.

The great need of this hour is for ten thousand preachers and teachers who are consumed with the character and personality of God! I'm not advocating imbalance, but it is the true knowledge of God that makes the rest of the message so significant. A church that has lost the knowledge of the incredible personality of God will be shallow, bored and passionless.

This is not a book filled with formulas, such as "how to achieve passionate Christianity in ten easy steps." Instead, it has to do with the powerful, concrete connection between *knowing* the truth about who God is and *experiencing* affection and passion in our hearts for Him. It is the revelation of God's passionate love and affection for us that awakens ever-deepening feelings of love and passion for Him. Simply put, we love Him because He first loved us (1 John 4:19).

Over and over Jesus said, "The kingdom of heaven is *at hand*" (Matt. 10:7, italics added). With that Scripture verse in mind, would you do something for me? Hold out your right hand in front of you.

Look at it. It's close, isn't it? So close you can stretch out your left hand and touch it.

The precious things of God are just that near to every child of God. They are *in our reach!* They are there for the taking. God is accessible. He has made Himself available. The question is, how much intimacy do we want? Just how passionate for Jesus do we want to be? You and I are the ones who set those limits, not God.

The promise of being transformed and ignited to holy passion by understanding and beholding God's glorious personality is for all believers. No matter how weak or strong we feel, regardless of our previous failures, irrespective of our natural temperaments or personalities, each of us can be ablaze with passion for Jesus.

If the first twenty years of my life taught me anything, it was that passion for Jesus does not come from natural human zeal or enthusiasm. Through frustration, condemnation and heartache, I realized what ignites a heart with passion. It can happen to anyone.

Let me tell you my story, how I started with human zeal and failed miserably. I want to show you how I gradually came to see God's affections and passions for me even in the midst of my many weaknesses. I believe you'll be strengthened in your passion for Jesus as you walk with me through the following pages.

ONE

The Roots of
Human Zeal

Come on, Rocky! Come on...492, 493, 494...." I could hear his raspy voice shouting encouragement and feel his thick hands grasping my ankles, keeping the calves of my legs pressed firmly against the floor.

"That's the way. Good! Good! You can do it! 496, 497, 498...Come on, son. All right! 500! 500! You did it again! I knew you had it in you, Rocky. That's my boy. See, all that hard work over the last several years is paying off, isn't it? Here, son, let me help you up. Dad wants to give you a hug."

I felt his huge forearms, hard as iron, squeezing the breath out of me. I could feel his warm breath on my cheek as he kissed me, feel his rough hands on my face, see his laughing eyes beaming into mine as he exclaimed, "Ten years old and doing five hundred sit-ups every day! No wonder the guys at Waldo's Tavern say you're gonna be a great athlete."

A tear splashed onto the article I'd been reading about my dad in the May 29, 1974, edition of *The Kansas City Times*, shattering my composure. Drying my eyes with the back of my hand, I continued reading once more, beginning with two paragraphs the reporter quoted from an article that had appeared in *The Times* on February 12, 1948, twenty-six years earlier:

> One of the greatest comebacks in the history of the 13th Golden Gloves Tournament of Champions was made last night.
>
> Bobby Bickle, a junior in Hoisington, Kansas, High School got off the floor in the second round to gain a well-earned verdict over Harold Stewart of Ft. Riley, Kansas, amid the wildest excitement of the approximately 7,000 fans.

Then the reporter continued his article which covered a third of the page:

> Bobby Bickle was the kind of man who refused to stay on the floor. In 1948 he fasted so relentlessly to make the featherweight class that he fainted twice at the weigh-in. Then he rose from the floor of the ring, dazed from a punch, and slugged his way to victory. He lost in the finals, but received the sportsmanship award of the 13th annual Tournament of Champions.
>
> As a lightweight, Bobby Bickle fought his way to the Kansas City Golden Gloves championship, the U.S. championship, and finally the international championship.

> Bobby Bickle is dead. He died yesterday at the
> age of 45, apparently of a heart attack....

The words before me dissolved once more in a blur of tears. Gone...the dearest person to me in all the world was gone. Yet what a legacy he had left me.

Dad was far from perfect as a man. He had many faults. Yet as far back as I could remember, I'd never met a person who knew my father and didn't admire and respect him. As a young, tough, amateur boxer, Dad had been known for his unbelievable discipline and devotion to his sport. His goal was to be an Olympic gold medalist and a world champion boxer. Consumed with zeal and driven by radical commitment to the sport he loved, he had worked out six to eight hours a day.

I couldn't recall whether it was in 1950 or 1951 that he'd become the amateur world champion while in the military. In 1952 he fought in the Olympics held in Helsinki, Finland. The night before his fight with the man who went on to win the gold medal, Dad broke his right hand in a bar fight. Disgusted with himself for allowing such a thing to happen, but fiercely determined to reach his goal, Dad fought the next day anyway — with one hand — and received a split decision. I'd heard his friends rave about that fight for years, listening in awe to their blow-by-blow descriptions of how my dad knocked the guy down three times in one round.

Failing to reach his lifelong dream hadn't defeated Dad or stolen his zeal. While in his twenties and fighting professionally, he was putting in eight hours a day on his job at the Chevrolet plant, then working out six to eight hours every day on top of that. The newspaper headline told it all: BOB BICKLE, CHAMPION OF COURAGE. Yes, that was my dad, all right.

I laid the paper on the kitchen table and sat down, alone with my thoughts. I was flooded with emotion as I pictured my father in my mind: his infectious grin; the nose that had been broken and reset too many times ever to look straight again; the scarred, blotchy eyebrows, split open so often he didn't even need Novocaine when they stitched them up because he had no nerves, no feeling there; that thick neck; those arms, solid as rocks, that had hugged me thousands of times.

Dad had been so physically and verbally affectionate with his children. It was as if he loved us so much he couldn't keep his hands off me and the six other kids in our family. He was always touching my face, loving on me, boxing and wrestling with me. He kissed us all many times. It was awesome. I loved it!

From my earliest memories way back when I was four years old, I could recall his telling me how great I was. He supported me 100 percent. It was easy to bounce back when I made mistakes because Dad was there for me. He had an incredible ability to overlook my failure because he saw my heart.

By the time I was five years old Dad was encouraging me to go to the Olympics. I didn't even know what the word meant at the time, but whatever the Olympics were, they excited my dad — so they excited me, too. He told me many stories of his good friends, Jack Dempsey and Floyd Patterson, both heavyweight world champions. Dad called me "Rocky" after the great fighter Rocky Marciano. He had me working out when I was six years old. By the time I was eight, I was working out several hours a day. Athletics seemed to come naturally for me. If Dad had wanted me to be a concert pianist, I'd have been in trouble for sure, but boxing seemed to be part of my nature. I enjoyed being encouraged in a sport I loved so dearly.

At ten years of age, my daily workout included running several miles, doing several hundred push-ups and five hundred sit-ups. Because of all the training and self-discipline, I had scores of school records right through high school for push-ups, sit-ups, running and other athletic accomplish-ments.

But I wasn't under some heavy burden to fulfill my dad's goals. I wasn't striving to make him happy. I felt he'd been happy with me all my life. I simply couldn't fail in his eyes. I enjoyed being with him so much that his goals just became my goals. I wanted to be just like him. Yet after training to be a boxer since I was six years old, at the age of fourteen I changed my mind and told Dad I'd rather play football. He never even blinked. Instantly he said, "That's great, son. I want you to do what is in your heart."

My dad and I had a tremendous friendship, filled with affirmation and love. He had confidence in me. He attended all my sporting events. If I was on the field, he was in the stands. While still only a sophomore in high school, I played on the sophomore football team, the junior varsity football team and the varsity football team — all at the same time. I played three games a week, and Dad never missed a one. His commitment to me was obvious to all who knew him. He'd even come and watch me at practices.

Dad was equally committed to my brother Pat, or "Punch," as Dad called him, who was just a year younger than I. We did much together.

When I was six or seven years old, he began working as a house painter. For years, nearly every weekend during school and all through the summers, Pat and I were right by his side, scraping peeling paint, cleaning brushes, scraping paint off windows and cleaning gutters.

From the time we were little kids, Dad took Pat and me to the bars with him, although he never let us drink. He was a real people person, laughing, joking and causing a commotion in a fun sort of way. As a result of being in the boxing world Dad hung around some pretty tough people. Some were Mafia-types with questionable ethics. Several of his friends whom I knew personally as a boy got shot and killed in the underground crime world.

Dad's friends were my friends. Here I was, a ten-year-old, strolling into bars beside my dad, "high-fiving" these guys twenty to forty years older than I and calling them by their first names. "Hey, Jim!" "Hi ya, Bill!" "Way to go, Orville!" I was one of the "buds." They told me dozens of Dad's old boxing stories, and I soon had them memorized down to the last detail. I liked the barmaids, too, because they mothered me and called me "Honey." Pat, Dad and I loved hanging out together in the bars, playing shuffleboard, shooting pool and playing the jukebox all day.

Although Pat and I enjoyed Waldo's Tavern, too, the place we visited most often was the VFW bar, a dingy, concrete block building that held maybe a hundred people. Every once in a while, Mom and our five sisters went along with us for the fish fry they had there every Friday night.

As we walked across the gravel parking lot, the air, always heavy with the aroma of frying fish and cigarette smoke, was filled with the warm, welcoming mixture of music from the jukebox, loud laughter, friendly chatter and the sound of guys playing pool. The sound level always seemed to escalate about fifty decibels when we walked through the door as Dad's friends there, blue-collared, tattooed, truck-driver types, called out greetings. Nobody ever bothered Dad. He was usually the toughest guy and the life of the party everywhere we went. People respected him for his eighteen years of boxing and all the championship titles he'd won.

IT NEVER OCCURRED TO us that bars weren't the best atmosphere for boys. None of our family went to church, although Dad told us there was a God. Neither of my parents was what anyone would term "religious."

When I was fourteen, something began stirring deep inside me. I'd always loved looking at the sky and stars, but now I felt an urge to figure out who was behind all the wonders of life. Sometimes I'd find myself staring up at the sky and mumbling, "There's got to be a God." So I went to my father with an unusual request. "Dad," I said, "I want to join a religion."

"That's good, son," he replied. "I think it's a great idea. I tried that myself once when I was younger. It'll be good for you."

"Yeah, I think so, too. But I don't know how to do it."

I could tell Dad was giving it a lot of thought. "I'll tell you what," he said. "If I were you, I'd be either a Jew or a Catholic. But you can make your own choice, because you have to choose your own religion."

"Oh," I said. "Why would you be either a Jew or a Catholic?"

"Because the Jews are richer, and the Catholics are bigger, more powerful in numbers and social influence worldwide. They seem to have high positions in society. But take your time and think about it. OK? Either one would be a good choice."

So I thought about it for a while. Then I came back and said, "Dad, I've made up my mind. I want to be a Jew. I'd rather be rich than big."

Dad smiled and caught me up in a big bear hug. "That's a good choice, son. Yes, sir. If I had it to do all over, I think I would have been a Jew."

"Dad, if I'm gonna be a Jew, how do I do it?"

"Tell you what, son. Look in the encyclopedia under 'Jews' and 'Judaism,' take some notes, bring them back to me, and we'll talk it over."

So I wrote up my little report and brought it back to him. It probably didn't make much sense, but he was enthusiastic. "That's good, Mike," he said.

"Now go to the synagogue down the road from our house and tell 'em you want to be a Jew."

When I walked into the synagogue, a service of some kind was going on so I sat down. Then I realized that everybody except me was wearing a little hat. I walked up to the rabbi after the service and introduced myself. "Hello," I said, extending my hand. "My name is Mike Bickle. I'm fourteen years old, and I want to be a Jew. How do I do it?"

I can't remember what the guy said, but he didn't seem excited about my decision, and he didn't communicate a lot of warmth or friendliness. So, a little dejected, I went back and told my dad, "I don't think they really want me to be a Jew so I'm going to be a Catholic."

I went back to the encyclopedia, read all about Catholicism and wrote out another little report for my dad. On Sunday I walked through our lower-income, run-down neighborhood to the Catholic church. As soon as the service ended, I took off for the front, past the railing, past what some regarded as a sacred boundary and right up to the pulpit. "Hello," I said as I shook the priest's hand. "I'm Mike Bickle, I'm fourteen years old, and I want to be a Catholic."

Putting his arm around me, the priest said, "Son, that's a great decision! I'll help you!" The priest's genuine excitement touched me: I felt so important in his eyes.

Father Tom Minges was in his thirties at the time. He made me feel right at home at St. Augustine's. For nearly a year, Father Minges met with me almost every Saturday afternoon at the rectory for an hour or so to teach me about the Catholic faith. What great times we had. He was a wonderful teacher. But for every new piece of information he gave me, I had ten questions. I had questions about God, questions about the Bible and questions about Catholicism. One day he sighed and said, "Son, we're never going to get through this if you don't quit asking so many questions."

Father Minges and I became good friends that year. He was so kind, and he always had time for me. I wasn't able to convert the entire junior high school to Catholicism as I'd hoped, but I did manage to get a few friends to go with me to church occasionally and to some of my studies with Father Minges. I loved being a Catholic, and I wanted them to be Catholics, too.

After a year, Father Minges decided I was ready to become a Catholic officially. Dad approved wholeheartedly, so I was confirmed and baptized. Was I excited! When my dad and I would go to the bars, he would always find one of his pals and say, "Hey, my son's a Catholic! Tell him, Mike. Tell him something about being a Catholic."

I told my story about being a Catholic so many times in those bars. Some of the old drunks would give me a dollar, hug me or pat me on the head and say, "Congratulations, Mike. You're a Catholic." It was serious business to me.

I WAS A SOPHOMORE in Center High School when my football coach Duane Unruh invited me to his home for a Bible study. "You'll love it, Mike," he said. "Other guys on the football team are members of the Fellowship of Christian Athletes, and they'll be there. We'll have a great time together."

"Sure," I said. "I'll come." I'm a Christian now, I thought to myself, and I'm supposed to go to Bible studies. Wonder why I never thought of that before?

Coach Unruh pursued me for Christ in a wise, tender way. Going to the home of the head varsity coach was an awesome thing for me, a little sophomore.

In June 1971, just before I turned sixteen, Coach Unruh invited me to a Fellowship of Christian Athletes summer camp at Estes Park, Colorado. If Coach had not paid my way, I never could have gone. My parents could never have afforded the luxury of a week-long camp. Roger Staubach, quarterback for the Dallas Cowboys, was to be the speaker. The night I boarded the bus transporting the campers from Kansas City to the camp, Dad gave me a warm hug and handed me a six-pack of beer. "Here, son," he said. "You'll need this." I shared it with all the guys on the bus.

Roger Staubach was great. Not only was he a tremendous speaker, but he was also very friendly to all the younger guys. What a tremendous role model he was, laughing and interacting with us. The poor guy had to throw hundreds and hundreds of passes to us that week. Each afternoon he'd meet us on the field and throw his famous, seventy-yard bombs.

When Staubach talked about his relationship with Jesus it was different from anything Father Minges and I had discussed. Although he'd taught me a lot about the importance of joining the church and loving God, and even about God loving me, I'd never heard anything like this. "You can be born again," Staubach told us. "You can have a personal relationship with Jesus Christ."

It was at that camp, on June 9, 1971, that I left all the guys, went off by myself and prayed a simple prayer that changed the course of my life. When I told Jesus I wanted to be born again and to have a personal relationship with Him, I suddenly felt the warmth of God in my heart. Although my experience with the Lord that day wasn't unusually dramatic or emotional, it did change me radically.

By the time the week was over and our bus took us home to Kansas City, I'd become a fiery evangelist, witnessing to everyone. I believed in hell. I believed in heaven. I believed God knew me. And I knew Him and wanted everyone to know Him. I didn't want anyone to go to hell.

I'd been home only a little while when the phone rang. It was Coach Unruh, wanting to know how the camp had been. He exploded with joy when I told him I'd met Jesus.

I thought my dad would be elated, too, but for the first time in my life I could tell he wasn't excited about what I'd done. He seemed bewildered and confused by my talk about hell, heaven and being born again.

But the thing that hit Dad the hardest was when I told him I couldn't go to the bars with him anymore. I even told him that if he and the guys in the bars didn't get saved, they were going to hell. I was a kid with no wisdom, and I seemed to judge everyone who did not immediately respond to Jesus. Even though Dad never vocalized it, I knew I'd hurt him, and that cut me to the quick. Although my dad's commitment to me never diminished, our communication was damaged to a certain degree from that time on.

When I got back from the camp in Colorado, I immediately began telling the guys on the football and track teams about Jesus. I was an outright fanatic by the time school opened in the fall of my junior year. I wore a nine-by-six-inch wooden cross around my neck because of the verse that said, "Carry your cross." I also lugged one of those six-inch-thick Catholic family Bibles to school. Although the athletes and students respected me, I knew I seemed weird to a lot of them. They couldn't understand what had happened to me. Students were whispering, "Bickle became a preacher. He got saved or something."

My older sister Sherry, a senior in high school, cried as she exclaimed to Mom and Dad, "You've got to make him quit. He's humiliating the whole family, carrying that giant Bible and wearing that big, wooden cross." She also knew I was witnessing in the school cafeteria. I'd usually choose an empty table, and every poor soul who came over to sit near me had to listen to my preaching. The Jesus movement was sweeping America then, and so many people were sensing a spiritual stirring, a hunger for God. I led many people to the Lord that first year or so after I was saved.

At the end of my first year as a Christian I received an invitation to live at the Colonial Presbyterian youth discipleship house. My father surprised me by agreeing with me that this would be a good opportunity for me to grow spiritually.

I was only sixteen, and most of those guys were college age or older. But they made me feel like one of them and began discipling me. They introduced me to the Bill Gothard seminars, Campus Crusade and the Navigators. I was hooked. I began attending Navigator and Crusade meetings, reading all their materials, studying the Bible and memorizing Scripture.

Nine of us lived together through the summer months. The church paid our room and board and gave us a small paycheck every week. We had many opportunities to share our faith and study the Bible. Two of the youth leaders from the Presbyterian church, Richard Beach and Bob Lehleitner, had become my faithful leaders, discipling me and strengthening my Christian walk. What a debt I will always owe those faithful men of God.

I graduated from high school, and in September 1973 I was off to Washington University in St. Louis. I was still witnessing to everyone who would listen. My pre-med studies were going great, I'd made the football team, and things couldn't have been any better. Then the ground seemed to drop right out from under my feet.

I'd been away at college almost a month when the phone rang late one Saturday evening. "Hey, Dad!" I said, thrilled to hear the familiar voice on the other end of the line. "How ya doin'? Did Center High's football team beat Oak Park tonight? How did Pat do?"

"Mike."

"Yeah, Dad?"

"Mike, Pat's had an accident...."

"Is he?... What happened? Is he gonna be all right?"

"We don't know, son. It looks pretty bad right now. It was just a normal high school football game, but somehow on one of the first plays of the game, Pat tackled the ball carrier and...He just lay there, Mike. I thought the wind had been knocked out of him or something, but he...he never moved. The coaches came pouring onto the field, and they called an ambulance. I...I thought we'd lost him, Mike."

"Where are you now, Dad?"

"Your mom and I are here at the North Kansas City Hospital. They won't let us in to be with Pat yet. They say they're still trying to get him stabilized and determine how much damage has been done."

"Dad, I'm coming. I'll be there just as quick as I can. Tell Mom I'll take the midnight train and be home by morning. I love you, Dad!"

The next morning, while sitting in a hospital waiting room, I read *The Kansas City Times* account of what had happened when my brother was injured:

> Again and again the memory comes back, no matter what Bob Bickle does to turn it off. The way he had just taken a seat in the stands and bought a couple of hot dogs. The speed with which it happened — in the second play of the game.
>
> And the way he just stood there on the sidelines with a lump in his throat, not wanting to go onto the field. Because his boy, Punch, looked dead. And then walking out there slowly, fists in his pockets, pushing through the others and looking down at the limp body in a football uniform.
>
> And the way his son said, "Hi, Dad." Then Bickle replied as though casually, "What's a matter, Punch?" With an effort to smile, the boy said, "I can't move."

My seventeen-year-old brother's neck was broken. In that split second as my 155-pound brother tried to tackle a 205-pound fullback, Pat had been transformed from an excellent athlete in perfect, vibrant health into a quadriplegic who couldn't move a finger. My brother even needed a respirator to help him breathe.

Pat had a broken neck, but my parents had broken hearts. Yet Mom still had our five sisters to take care of and a household to run, and Dad had to keep working to support the family. I knew the thing for me to do was to forget college for a while, go home and help take care of my brother.

So by October 1, 1973, just a month after leaving home, I was back in Kansas City. Pat's doctors told Mom and Dad he needed to go to the Craig Rehabilitation Institute in Denver. As soon as all the arrangements were made, Pat and I had left for Colorado.

Soon after Pat and I left for Denver, the people of Kansas City planned a fund-raiser for Pat and my family. A reporter for *The Times* recalled the event.

> A double-header benefit game at Arrowhead Stadium, Nov. 17, raised $43,464. A lot of money, but expenses were and are high.
>
> Bobby Bickle was there that night with his wife, Peggy. Bob Bickle stood in the glare of the stadium lights and looked out at the 20,000 persons who had attended the game. He thought of the Kansas City community that had rallied to the support of his son. The children who had sent pennies and nickels. The bankers and businessmen and football players and workers and farmers and people from every walk of life who had been there when they were needed.
>
> His eyes began to shine in the lights' glare. A powerful face moved to tears. "Man," he said roughly, "this is the greatest city in the world....Somebody needs to write a book about this city."

Pat and I stayed at the rehab center a little over four months so he could undergo physical therapy, and I could be trained to give him total care. The nurses and therapists taught me how to feed and bathe Pat, how to make his bed and how to turn him every two hours or so to help keep him from getting pneumonia or developing bed sores. They also showed me how to brush his teeth, how to exercise his muscles and give him the medication he required.

At first, Pat held up really well. Man, was he tough. What a fighter! But as the reality of it all began to hit him, I could see so many questions and such emotional pain in my brother's eyes. I didn't think I could stand the pain I felt for Pat at times, but I tried to keep up his spirits.

During the following months when Dad phoned or came to visit, we had some good, long talks. He thanked me for helping lift the load that had simply been too much for him to carry alone.

One evening as we chatted, Dad's tone grew strangely solemn. "I know you're only eighteen, Mike, and that's young to carry such responsibilities." Dad hesitated, groping for words. "Mike," he said, putting his hand on my shoulder, "I know you love God. Will you promise me before your God that if anything happens to me, you will take care of your brother for the rest of his life?"

Although Dad seemed so sober, so intensely serious, the thought of anything ever happening to my father was inconceivable. He was forty-five years old and in the prime of life. But I knew he was wise to make sure all the bases were covered — just in case. I reached up and clasped his rough hand in both of mine. "Yes, Dad," I said soberly. "I promise before my God to lovingly and joyfully take care of Pat all the days of my life." I meant it with all my heart, and Dad knew it. I could sense peace and relief settling over my father like a blanket.

Late in May, Dad and I brought Pat back to Denver for a second series of treatments. "Son," he said, "if it's all right with you, I'd like to drive over to Fraser, Colorado, and visit my uncle. I won't be gone more than one day. Maybe the little drive into the mountains will help clear my head."

"Sure, Dad. Just take your time. Pat and I are fine. Stay as long as you like." I got up from the chair beside Pat's bed and walked Dad to the door. I knew he felt torn emotionally, seeing Pat in such distress and turmoil. His face looked so drawn, so tired.

Just as my father turned to walk out the door, I stopped him. Looking him straight in the eyes, I said, "Dad, I love you!"

He flashed that broad smile of his that could light up a

room. "Son," he said, "I love you, and I'm *so proud* of you."
Dad had always been proud of me.

Those were the last words my father ever spoke to me. On
his way into the mountains, he had a heart attack and died.

As I finished reading the newspaper article about my
father's death, I folded the paper carefully and tucked it
under my arm. Somehow it was a link with the most special
person I'd ever known, and I wanted to keep it always.
Walking over to the window, I leaned my forehead against
the cold glass, even though I couldn't see anything through
my tears.

"Good-bye, Dad," I wept. "I love you, and I'll always love
you. Don't worry. I'll keep my vow. I'll lovingly and joyfully
take care of Pat for his entire life."

In my heart I imagined Dad cheering me on, one last time:
That's my boy! I know you're gonna make it, Mike! Oh, son,
I'm so proud of you!

TWO

When Human Zeal
Is Not Enough

With my father gone, a new weight of responsibility seemed to drop on my shoulders. For a while, Mom just "spun out" emotionally. None of us kids had much trouble understanding why. Only God knows the aching emptiness she faced night and day with Dad suddenly gone.

There she was, a young widow with only a high-school education and a totally paralyzed son, five daughters and me to provide for. My older sister Sherry was nineteen; I was eighteen; Pat was seventeen; the twins, Shelly and Kelly, were fifteen; Tracey was fourteen; and Lisa was eleven. When my sisters and I saw what was happening to Mom, we all pulled together to try to make her burden lighter. I learned then that my sisters were the best anyone could ever have.

Fifteen years later, when Mom confided that Dad had battled a terminal heart disease for three years before his fatal heart attack but hadn't wanted anyone to know, I understood things a little better. She said that every night for nine months, from the time of Pat's accident in September until May when Dad died, he had wept when he went to bed. He'd loved Pat so much, and the thought of his son's being a quadriplegic for life grieved him deeply. Mom said the doctors had already warned Dad before Pat's accident that his heart couldn't last much longer.

I didn't know all that at age eighteen, but I was so glad my father had possessed the wisdom and courage to talk to me about assuming responsibility for Pat's care. How that conversation with me must have crushed him, knowing he was soon to die and that he'd be leaving a paralyzed son and a large, young family. I was determined to keep my promise, but at about the nine-month mark of Pat's 'round-the-clock care things really started sliding downhill. Dad's death, on top of Pat's own paralysis, seemed to be more than my brother could handle. It became harder and harder to get a smile out of him. I watched helplessly as the light in his eyes, once fueled by hope and determination, slowly flickered and went out.

Day-to-day existence became more bitter than death for Pat. He seemed to hate life with a passion. By the one-year mark following his accident, my brother despised every moment of life — every breath. He was consumed with bitterness and frustration. Nothing was right. He was totally paralyzed, totally helpless and totally hopeless. He saw my face nearly twenty-four hours a day. That in itself was pretty depressing to him. Every two hours — even through the night — I was touching him, turning him, helping to sustain the existence he utterly loathed. And so he took part of his frustration and anger out on me and on all the others around him.

The doctors and nurses had warned me that such a thing

often happens as an individual works through the various stages of grief. The paralysis alone was more than most people could have handled. Yet Pat, who had loved Dad as I did, was having to deal with the grief of losing him. His sorrow was just as bitter as mine, and he had to bear it while simultaneously confronting all the fears and frustrations accompanying paralysis. I knew my brother's reaction was perfectly normal, but that knowledge didn't make things any easier.

At two in the morning, as I struggled, half asleep, to turn Pat or give him a sip of water, I'd be met with angry, stinging words: "You jerk! You idiot! Can't you do anything right?" I never knew when he was going to give vent to his seething inner turmoil.

I was not upset by Pat's words at first, but gradually I began returning them with haughty, sarcastic remarks of my own. I literally wanted to punch his lights out. Anger sometimes rose in my heart to the point that I'd have to walk out of the room for a while and cool off just to keep from slapping him silly. Even thinking such a thing shook me to the core. Imagine being tempted to slap my paralyzed brother!

I experienced intense guilt over the unloving feelings I harbored toward Pat. He had always been so special to me. I felt like a total failure because of my obvious lack of love and graciousness. Serving others was supposed to be one of the hallmarks of genuine spirituality, yet I was failing at every turn. How could a real Christian feel as angry, selfish and loveless as I did? I'd made a vow to my dad, and to God, that I'd *joyfully* and *lovingly* take care of Pat all the days of my life. Yet in less than a year and a half things had already degenerated to the place that I complained continually, was immersed in self-pity and sometimes could barely stand to be in the same room with him. I was spending all my days and nights at his bedside; but Pat didn't even seem to care. His emotional pain was so great that he couldn't see the pain of those around him.

By this time, Mom was beginning to pull herself together again, little by little. She saw what was happening and realized that Pat and I both needed some sort of change. So in September 1974 I enrolled at the University of Missouri, a two-hour drive from our house. I still came home and cared for Pat from Friday afternoon through Sunday during my one year at the university. The change did us both good, and within a short time Pat's anger and frustration peaked and began to subside.

I was enjoying my year at the university. I liked the classes and enjoyed the fellowship of my three Christian roommates. I studied hard, hitchhiking home to take care of Pat at the end of each week and still giving it everything I had spiritually. Drawing on the resource of natural human zeal imparted by my father, I was witnessing to at least one person each day; studying and memorizing the Word; and diligently scheduling my time, including an hour for prayer every evening.

The year before, I'd been captured by Leonard Ravenhill's book *Why Revival Tarries*. One of Ravenhill's statements plagued me: "Any leader who refuses to pray two hours a day will not be worth a plug nickel in preaching." That sentence stabbed my heart like a knife. I believed Ravenhill was right, so I had promised myself I'd begin with an hour of prayer a day and work up to two as I could. I was keeping that promise.

Weary to the bone and emotionally and spiritually exhausted as well, I finally "hit the wall." Here was my little brother, who had been blasted with twice the grief I'd been called to endure, and he was working through his like a champ. On the other end of the scale, there I was with the unresolved pain of my father's death still throbbing in my heart, still struggling to mask my feelings and continuing to experience anger in my heart toward anyone who required me to serve them.

For the first time, I was also facing tremendous guilt before

God over several other areas of failure in my spiritual life. I missed my Dad's affirming, unconditional love, but I doubted that God would ever love me like that. After all, I'd never failed my dad in the way I felt I was failing God. My heart seemed as hard as a rock and spiritually dull. I felt neither passion for God nor tenderness toward others. I was also beginning to despise the commitments I'd made to spiritual disciplines.

More than anything, I wanted to please God; yet I had suddenly found myself failing Him at every turn: I — Mike Bickle, the "Wonder Boy," who had never really failed at anything. I'd never used drugs, not even once. Never smoked a cigarette in my life. I'd drunk a few beers once on my trip to the summer camp, but I'd never messed around with any of the wild women at college who seemed to be in abundance everywhere.

I'd usually achieved my goals in everything I attempted athletically, academically and spiritually: setting school records, making straight A's all through high school, praying, studying my Bible, winning people to the Lord and memorizing Scripture. By the time I turned eighteen, I'd memorized many chapters of the Bible. I was praying at least an hour a day, and the previous year when I wasn't in college, I had studied the Bible six to eight hours every day while sitting at my brother's bedside. I was fasting regularly and keeping the promise I'd made to myself to witness to at least one person every day. I didn't realize it then, but the ingredients for an angry, self-righteous Pharisee were all in place. I was drifting away from God emotionally, even though my outward spiritual disciplines concealed the growing chasm.

The same human zeal my dad had possessed had also consumed me for as long as I could remember. But suddenly, for the first time in my life, zeal was not enough. If anything, it had turned on me and become my enemy — taunting me with accusations regarding my imperfections and condemning me for my miserable spiritual failures. I was being

knocked down and defeated by my total inability to overcome anger, walk in genuine love and develop real affection
for God. Mike Bickle, who had seemed able to confront and
change so many things, couldn't even change his own heart.

Here I was, nineteen years old, and I felt like one big
mess, one huge spiritual failure. Denying that fact was use-
less. I knew it, and I feared that the God I so earnestly
longed to please knew it too. What must He be thinking of
me? I could picture the anger, the disappointment, the frustration that must be on His face.

I was failing at the one and only vow I'd ever made to my
dad or my God. How could I ever expect to care for Pat
lovingly and joyfully all the days of my life when I couldn't
even relate to Jesus lovingly and joyfully? Shocked and disappointed by the sin in my heart — impatience, self-righteousness, unforgiveness, anger, self-pity and lack of
self-control — I couldn't even look at myself in the mirror,
much less try to look God "in the eye" when I talked to Him
in prayer. My Christian friends assured me that the Lord
loved me, but *they* couldn't see my heart the way God and I
could. My spirit was beginning to close to God because of
my legalism, guilt and fear of divine rejection. I had lost the
sense of freshness that comes when our spirits are open
through bold confidence in God's tender grace.

I was also failing at prayer. Oh, I continued to pray an
hour a day — by the clock. But I *despised*, absolutely *despised* it. What drudgery. How could I ever conclude that I
loved God when I so disliked praying to Him? Sure, there
were a few times when I broke through into God's presence.
But, in my heart, I actually wondered if watching the clock
and praying uninspired prayers that seemed to tumble right
off my lips and hit the floor were really doing any good.
Frankly, many of the hours I spent on my knees seemed like
a miserable waste of precious time.

I was beginning to despise witnessing, too. The powerful
Jesus movement that had been sweeping the nation during

my last two years in high school and first year of college was waning. Determined to keep my solemn commitment to witness to at least one person every day, I still talked to many people, but with very meager results.

Late one evening I went to bed frustrated because I hadn't spoken to anyone about the Lord all day. After midnight, I forced myself out of bed, got dressed and wandered around the university campus until I found someone with whom I could share my faith. I gave the individual a short, almost angry account of salvation, then rushed back to bed muttering, "This can't be how I live the rest of my spiritual life!" Witnessing had become dead, dry and ritualistic. I had become angry at God.

I was failing in my vow to take care of Pat and failing in prayer. Now I could chalk up failure number three — I was a terrible witness.

I probably couldn't have verbalized it at the time, but I had stumbled headlong into an important principle: Self-righteous, human zeal is sure to fail, and the fallout eventually produced by that failure is guilt and religious anger toward God and people.

Then, of course, there was Bible study. What a drag that was becoming. My zeal to be a radical, on-fire believer was still high, but my inward affection for the Lord and for His Word had grown so cold. I was still attending Navigator and Campus Crusade meetings, studying through the New Testament book by book with various commentaries, but everything seemed so dead and dull. My head knowledge was growing, but my heart seemed to be shrinking by the day. Instead of becoming more enlightened, I was growing more and more confused. Spiritual things had become so sterile — barren, wearisome and tedious.

I was failing at fasting, too. I broke my regular commitment to fast so many times in the middle of the "fast day" that it was pitiful. I hated fasting.

I was almost twenty years old by this time — and nothing

but a ball of frustration because I viewed myself as a spiritual failure. And the failure crushing the life out of me was in the spiritual things I cared the most intensely about — not in drinking or carousing. I was coming to the place where I felt like quitting totally, because I'd finally realized I simply was not capable of loving Jesus as I felt I should. In my quest to love and please God, I had aspired to His holy standards but had fallen miserably short.

My initial ideas of God's loving affections for me had faded almost to the point of nonexistence. If I was a total failure and disappointment in my own eyes, I shuddered to think how I must look in the eyes of my God who had been so kind, so very good, to me. How could He even like me? How could He stand to look at me when I was failing so terribly? Surely He no longer enjoyed my fellowship with Him.

A Startling Thought

One evening as I was reading the Scriptures, a passage from the fifth chapter of John hit my heart like a bolt of lightning.

> You search the Scriptures, because you think that in them you have eternal life; and it is these that bear witness of Me; and *you are unwilling to come to Me, that you may have life* (John 5:39-40, italics added).

I suddenly realized I was like the pious Pharisees who studied the Scriptures day and night, yet didn't enjoy an affectionate relationship with the *person* those very Scriptures were about. Like the Pharisees, I had been studying words on paper instead of cultivating an intimate relationship with a person, and my heart had been growing colder and colder toward God.

Certain that my failure and immaturity must be angering the heart of God, I had feared He might be ready to toss me on the junk heap as a total loss and turn His attention elsewhere. Time after time, I'd found myself wishing my dad were still alive to provide the unconditional affection to which I'd grown so accustomed. I could imagine him running to me with open arms and a giant grin.

Then one day as I was reading the story of the prodigal son — a portion of Scripture I'd gone over who knows how many times in the past, the verbs regarding the prodigal's father suddenly came alive: "And he got up and came to his father. But while he was still a long way off, his father *saw* him, and *felt compassion* for him, and *ran* and *embraced* him, and *kissed* him" (Luke 15:20, italics added).

In the midst of my spiritual coldness and failure I had wondered so many times how God felt about me. I'd even dreaded to imagine the expression on His face when He saw me coming back for forgiveness each time I let Him down. Suddenly I knew, for through the prodigal's father I glimpsed the face and heart of God. When God saw me trudging toward His throne with my head bowed in shame, like the prodigal's father, He was moved with affection and tenderness for me. He was running toward me with joy and excitement. His arms were outstretched, reaching for me, longing to catch me up in His loving embrace and kiss away my guilt and failure.

My heavenly Father was a watching, running, weeping, laughing, embracing, kissing God! He was an encouraging, affirming, praising, affectionate kind of God. He was a God who loved me so much He couldn't keep from embracing me. I was the apple of His eye. He was a God who loved my friendship and just wanted me to be with Him. A Father who bragged on me to anyone who would listen. A God who enjoyed me even in my failure and immaturity because He saw the sincere intentions of my heart. A God I didn't have to strive to make happy, because He'd been happy with me from the second I was born into His family. He was a Father who was always cheering me on from the sidelines. He enthusiastically called me His son.

The awesome truth came streaking across my soul, bursting in beautiful splendor, lighting up my heart with this truth! How could I have missed it? For years I'd been struggling to please God and come up to His "expectations," when all along my heavenly Father had loved me *as my dad loved me* — only a million times more! My heavenly Father was so much more affectionate than even my earthly father. If I could measure His love, it would be "as high as the heavens are above the earth" (Ps. 103:11, NIV). From that moment, my new understanding of God's extravagant affections for me began to change my life powerfully and radically, replacing my guilt with holy boldness and passionate affections for Him.

Sincere Intention Versus Mature Attainment

During those past few years, in my zeal to please God and be like Him, I had run into His holiness. I was encountering my own sin and weakness, awakening to my total inability to change my own heart. In short, I, like the apostle Paul, had come face-to-face with my own human weakness (Rom. 7).

I thought of Paul, a zealous personality who was transformed and filled with holy passion as a result of seeing the splendor of God's personality. For the surpassing value of knowing a glorious *person*, Paul counted all things but rubbish in order that he might gain Christ (Phil. 3:6-9).

I realized that I, like the erring nation of Israel, had possessed an enthusiastic but totally unenlightened zeal for God (Rom. 10:2-3). All my human zeal had been able to produce was a perfectionistic performance mentality and merciless self-condemnation which resulted in religious anger filling my heart. I had been struggling earnestly to reach the top of the ladder of works and self-righteousness. But when I looked up, I realized that the top of the ladder, still far beyond my grasp, was leaning against an insurmountable wall of guilt, frustration and powerlessness.

I had been living under crushing condemnation, struggling under the painful misconception that God had judged me by my attainments and thus rejected me. Yet, while I had been focusing on my lack of mature attainment, God had been looking at my sincere intentions. He hadn't been pacing impatiently back and forth in front of His throne, moaning and covering His face in despair or throwing up His hands in frustration every time I stumbled. He had been looking at my earnest desires and my responsive heart that said, "I want to do Your will," and He was delighting in me. I was beginning to understand His overwhelming affection for me, even in the midst of my spiritual immaturity.

The Father-heart of God was as thrilled with me — an immature, mess-making, spiritual infant — as with one of His spiritually mature sons who had just graduated with honors from the school of the Spirit. My heavenly Father was enjoying me while I was yet in the *process* of maturing, not sighing in disgust and waiting impatiently until I grew up. He loved and longed for me; He felt proud and was excited over me even while I was falling short.

Oh, the sense of anticipation and excitement that filled my heart as I realized my Lord and I could have a tremendous friendship; such affirmation and affection; such love for each other; and such tremendous confidence in one another. It was too good to be true! I wept for joy. And when the tears finally ceased, I could sense the anger, bitterness, guilt and condemnation melting away. My heart felt so different. As my confidence in Him grew, my heart became soft and pliable, fervent and warm. Understanding God's great affection for me ignited my love for Him. My little, flickering flame of human zeal was replaced by a consuming blaze of passionate love for a glorious *person*. His intense devotion and ardent affection for me far exceeded that of my earthly father's...and I knew I would never, ever, be the same.

THREE

Is Your God
Too Small?

Idol worship? I never would have believed anything could have made me bow down and worship before an idol. Well, it wasn't an idol exactly. Actually, it was a...no, I think I'd better start at the beginning.

It was the spring of 1972, and since the first of the year I had already seen *The Ten Commandments* starring Charlton Heston about ten times at the local drive-in movie theater. I was totally awed by Moses' encounter with God at the burning bush, and after seeing the movie I'd read the book of Exodus over and over. My favorite part was God's warning to Moses: "No man can see Me and live!" (Ex. 33:20). I quoted

43

that verse every time I got a chance in my high school Bible study groups, assuring my friends that it was true and God really meant business. They all listened soberly, even though one buddy cautioned that the verse seemed a little too heavy to have as my favorite, all-time Scripture verse.

During my "burning bush" phase, our Presbyterian youth group drove down to Dallas, Texas, to see Billy Graham and hear him preach to 120,000 people at Campus Crusade's week-long event called "Expo '72." His sermons about the cost of discipleship challenged his hearers to evangelize the entire world. Fired by Graham's powerful messages, my friend Steve and I were absolutely convinced that we had heard God tell us to go to Africa. As missionaries we would evangelize that heathen nation. The bad part was that we planned to leave in August — giving me only two months to get ready.

We were juniors in high school with no financial backing, no direction and no training. But the fact that we were both only sixteen years old was of little concern to us. We were convinced that God had called us, just as He had called Moses in *The Ten Commandments*. What we lacked in money and wisdom, we would make up for in youthful zeal. While driving back to Kansas City, Steve and I planned out the missionary strategies we would use to convert Africa.

It was already past 10:00 P.M. when Steve and I arrived at the Colonial Presbyterian Discipleship House where we were living that summer with eight other guys. They hadn't made it back from Dallas yet. We were tired and didn't feel like waiting up for them. We undressed and turned out the light. Groping our way across the pitch-black basement we all used as our bedroom, Steve and I wearily went to bed.

"Before we go to sleep, let's commit ourselves to God one more time to go to the mission fields of Africa," I urged piously. Closing our eyes, we each took a turn leading aloud in prayer. "Oh, God," I prayed fervently, "we will surely go. I know how much Africa needs us. We know we are not yet fully trained, but neither was Moses. Oh, God, please confirm this to us."

Steve and I opened our eyes and without the slightest warning, we both beheld a most unusual sight. A brilliant, glowing light appeared directly across the room just inches off the floor. I could almost swear it was blazing as brightly as the burning bush at the drive-in movie theater. Surely this was the confirmation we'd prayed for. "It must be God!" I whispered excitedly.

Awestruck and trembling in fear, Steve and I crept out of bed and crawled across the floor toward the fire. "Don't look, Steve!" I whispered, sounding the same warning I'd repeated to him so many times: "Don't ever look at God, or you'll surely die!" In whispered tones Steve assured me he understood the principle.

We crawled toward the light, then knelt side by side and covered our eyes with our hands. Through the cracks between our fingers we could still see the glow of the flickering, mysterious fire.

"Oh, God," I whispered, "send us to Africa."

Hardly daring to breathe, we awaited God's response. Several minutes passed, but we were met with nothing but silence. "Please don't look," I said again in Steve's direction, "or you will surely die!"

Once more, Steve assured me he understood. The seconds dragged by. "What shall we do now, Mike?" he asked softly.

"Pray a little louder this time, just in case."

Steve prayed, and we waited. When there was no response, we each took a turn or two at quoting different verses from the Bible. Again, we were met with silence.

I even tried imitating the British accent of one of my favorite preachers, Stephen Olford, as I prayed and quoted Isaiah 6:8, "Here am I. Send me," but nothing seemed to be working. Finally, Steve could stand the suspense no longer.

He peeked.

Instantly, Steve let out a hair-raising scream and fell over on top of me, sending me sprawling. Hadn't I warned him not to peek? Now the Lord had killed him for sure.

As I fell in a heap, I opened one eye and then the other. To my horror, I saw an ordinary, old water heater whose pilot flame — probably much to God's holy amusement — had kicked on at the precise moment we'd asked the Lord for a sign. I didn't even know the water heater was in the closet because it had been hidden behind some clothes. One of our roommates had moved out the week we were out of town. Behind all his clothes stood the water heater, previously invisible to would-be worshippers.

Embarrassed beyond words, Steve and I collapsed on the floor, promising each other we'd never tell the story. But it was too good to keep. You'd be hard-pressed to convince either of us that God doesn't have a sense of humor.

Neither Steve nor I went to Africa that summer. After the episode of bowing down to the water heater, we opted to stay in Kansas City and finish our senior year in high school.

AS YOUNG CHRISTIANS WE misunderstood a lot of things. We were not supposed to go to Africa — at least not as juniors in high school. Our burning bush experience was only a water heater. But there was one thing we got right: The glory of God is beyond anything we've ever imagined. Since my teenage years I've been gripped with a yearning to see Him, to have a heart after Him and to grow in the knowledge of God.

While in my teens I discovered books such as *The Knowledge of the Holy* by A. W. Tozer, *Gleanings in the Godhead* by Arthur W. Pink and *Knowing God* by J. I. Packer. I devoured them from cover to cover. My heart was warmed by the holy fire that blazed in the souls of these men who seemed to know the splendor and majesty of God so intimately.

It is the knowledge of the holy One that fires the heart with passion. I kept reading my Bible and those three books over and over. As I read, meditated and prayed, the Holy

Spirit took the hammer of truth and began breaking up some of the inferior, inadequate concepts of God that had been built into my life. He began to lay a new foundation, and the process is still going on to this day. My inner man is continually in the process of being renewed into a fuller, more complete knowledge of God and His glorious personality.

We individual believers and the church as a whole possess so little of the knowledge of what God is truly like. Our ignorance of His diverse and glorious personality rots our religion. It leads to errors in our doctrines and contributes to the decay of our confidence and passion in worship. Our inadequate ideas about the personhood of God result in failure to develop deep affection for Jesus and to obey Him with fearless abandonment. Our faulty religious ideas of God damage our relationships with Him, deplete our prayer lives and drain the joy from our sacrificial service.

J. I. Packer correctly diagnosed this great disease in the church when he wrote:

> Christian minds have been conformed to the modern spirit: the spirit...that spawns great thoughts of man and leaves room for only small thoughts of God.[1]

How Big Is Your God?

Our world is affected tragically every day by people who possess little or no sense of God's transcendence. Much of creation does not know — or care — that its Creator is unequalled, unrivaled and supreme. *Transcendence* when in reference to God means that He exists, not only in, but beyond our realm of reality. In other words, He's not like us — far from it. God is exalted far above His created universe, so far that even the brightest human minds cannot begin to fathom it. As Tozer explains:

The caterpillar and the archangel, though far removed from each other in the scale of created
things, are nevertheless one in that they are alike
created. They both belong in the category of that-
which-is-not-God and are separated from God by
infinitude itself.[2]

In Old Testament times, whenever God appeared to men,
an overwhelming sense of terror and dread was the result.
When God spoke to Abram, His beloved friend fell on his
face (Gen. 17:3). When the Angel of the Lord appeared to
Moses in a flame of fire out of the midst of a bush, Moses hid
his face, for he was afraid to look at God (Ex. 3:2-6).

In contrast, many in our day are so blind to God's
transcendence that they show shocking disregard for Him.
If people are unaware of God's awesome superiority and
supremacy that transcend this universe and time itself,
they will have little fear of Him. If we have no fear of God,
the fear of consequences is no longer a deterrent, and we
will break His decrees without hesitation. The downward
spiral of morality in our society is directly proportional to
the loss of our understanding of the greatness of God. In
the minds of most people who believe there is a God, He
is only a little more than an elected official — not to be
taken too seriously.

Why does our society have such a limited and irreverent
view of God? The answer is simple. The church has not
proclaimed it! The church's concept of God is also too small.

For many Christians Jesus is more like Santa Claus or a pop
psychologist than the holy Other who will judge heaven and
earth by His word.

The glory of God's personhood has not been revealed fully
to our generation. But when the faintest light of God's surpassing greatness dawns upon our minds, we will know
what it means to walk softly before the Lord and to work out
our salvation with fear and trembling.

Daniel, a man greatly beloved by God, was granted an overpowering vision:

> His body also was like beryl, his face had the appearance of lightning, his eyes were like flaming torches, his arms and feet like the gleam of polished bronze, and the sound of his words like the sound of a tumult. Now I, Daniel, alone saw the vision, while the men who were with me did not see the vision; nevertheless, a great dread fell on them, and they ran away to hide themselves. So I was left alone and saw this great vision; yet no strength was left in me, for my natural color turned to a deathly pallor, and I retained no strength...Then behold, a hand touched me and set me trembling on my hands and knees (Dan. 10:6-8,10).

Daniel was left speechless and breathless, and all his strength was drained from him (Dan. 10:15,17). In the vision he was told that the Lord had sent Michael, the archangel, to fight with the demonic prince of Persia. The messenger in the vision Daniel saw was only another lower-ranked angel. What would it have been like to have beheld Michael or even the Lord Himself? Without doubt such revelation would change our thinking about a lot of things. Our worship will be ignited with passion.

When we begin to comprehend the excellencies of God's person, we will be horrified by the declining ethics and decaying morality in our churches and our nation. Whether by insight and spiritual revelation or by visions in Technicolor, the effect is the same. Beholding the holiness and glory of God reveals the presence of sin and its terrible ugliness.

Isaiah was probably the most righteous man in all Israel in his day. He was the prophet of God. Notice his response after seeing a vision of the Lord sitting on His throne:

Then I said,
"Woe is me, for I am ruined!
Because I am a man of unclean lips,
And I live among a people of unclean lips;
For my eyes have seen the King, the Lord of
    hosts" (Is. 6:5).

A new revelation of God's holiness always shines the spotlight on our own condition.

No Contradictions With God

Small thoughts about the personhood of God hinder an intimate relationship with Him. Our ignorance of God's personality has also led to errors in the theology and doctrine of the church. The average believer is intimidated at times by words like *theology* and *doctrine* because they sound so intellectual and controversial.

Theology is simply the study of God and His relationship with man and the universe. And doctrine is what is taught as the belief of a church. You cannot cast off theology and doctrine in order to be "simply Christian."

Incorrect views of God can create confusion and misunderstanding. For example, our imperfect knowledge of God has sometimes led us to imagine Him in conflict with Himself — His long-suffering tugging against His wrath, or His justice wrestling against His mercy. As Tozer says, "Between His attributes no contradiction can exist. He need not suspend one to exercise another, for in Him all His attributes are one."[3]

If only more believers understood that God is immutable — He never changes. What He has always been, He will ever be. God never suspends one attribute to exercise another. For example, He never diminishes in His holiness when He exercises His love and mercy. None of God's qualities ever diminishes in even the slightest degree.

In fact, when one immutable aspect of the nature of God is seemingly in conflict with another of His immutable attributes, it is at that place you will see glimpses of His greatness.

Suppose there was a gardener who had planted and cared for a prize-winning bed of flowers. He would spare no expense. Which would the gardener hate more: a weed in the common field or a weed in the bed of his prize flowers? Obviously, he would hate the weed in his flower bed more because it chokes the life out of his prize flowers and destroys the glory of his handiwork.

In the same way God hates all sin. Nothing describes His abhorrence for sin in the wicked better than the degree of eternal punishment He prescribes for it. Nevertheless, He hates sin infinitely more in the lives of Christians because we are His vineyard, "the plantings of the Lord" (Is. 61:3). The most wonderful thing of all is that He loves us with an everlasting love and reckons us as perfectly righteous because of our faith in Christ and His work on the cross.

I hate the sin of lying. But I would hate it so much more if it were found in one of my own sons. Why? Because I am their father. I love them, and they are called by my name.

When you begin to comprehend God's perfect and immutable holiness, and at the same time realize His unfathomable love for you, you will understand His hatred of sin in your life. The illumination of our hearts with the knowledge of God transforms us into that same image. A casual attitude about sin comes from an incomplete understanding of God.

The cross of Calvary was the greatest display of the character and attributes of God. God in His perfect holiness does not wink at the slightest sin. He did not say to Adam, "That's one! Don't let it happen again." It was for that one act of disobedience that Adam and all his race fell.

I have often been asked, "If God is a God of love, how could He send anyone to hell?" But the more appropriate question is this: If God is a God of perfect holiness, how could He send anyone to heaven?

How can a holy and just God arbitrarily overlook sin? How could a loving God not forgive them? Immutable holiness and unconditional love collide. But God would never violate His holiness nor turn away from His love. The greatness of God was displayed, not in the fact that He forgave our sins, but in precisely *the way* He forgave them — He sent His Son as a perfect sacrifice for us. His love was displayed, and His justice was satisfied. The apostle Paul said in his letter to the Romans that in the cross God became both the just and the justifier of the one who has faith in Jesus (Rom. 3:26).

Some have such a dim view or low appreciation for both the holiness and love of God that the cross doesn't seem that significant. They understand neither the greatness of their need nor the glory of God's gift.

Jesus taught that the one who has been forgiven much will love much (Luke 7:47). You will "love much" when you begin to comprehend the magnitude of what Christ has done on your behalf. Passion is birthed in you by revelation of the knowledge of God.

Our Prayer Lives

An imperfect understanding of God's immutability has decreased the quality of prayer for many Christians and has led to misunderstandings regarding the nature of prayer. We cannot "twist God's arm" or throw a temper tantrum to make Him give us what we want. A wise earthly father does not respond to such tactics, and neither does our heavenly Father.

A more accurate understanding of the goodness of God can also be a tremendous aid to prayer. It is God's goodness, not ours, that is the basis for blessing. Understanding this frees us to place our confidence and trust in God Himself instead of being forced to rely upon our own righteousness or upon whatever faith we can muster. As Tozer said:

There can be no merit in human conduct, not even in the purest and the best. Always God's goodness is the ground of our expectation. Repentance, although necessary, is not meritorious but a condition for receiving the gracious gift of pardon which God gives of His goodness. Prayer is not in itself meritorious. It lays God under no obligation nor puts Him in debt to any. He hears prayer because He is good, and for no other reason. Nor is faith meritorious; it is simply confidence in the goodness of God, and the lack of it is a reflection upon God's holy character.

The whole outlook of mankind might be changed if we could all believe that we dwell under a friendly sky and that the God of heaven, although exalted in power and majesty, is eager to be friends with us.

...The greatness of God rouses fear within us, but His goodness encourages us not to be afraid of Him. To fear and not be afraid — that is the paradox of faith.[4]

I saw a Dennis the Menace cartoon one time that illustrates these points. Dennis and his friend were walking out of Mrs. Wilson's house with cookies in both hands. Dennis's friend wondered what they had done to deserve the cookies. Dennis explained, "Mrs. Wilson doesn't give us cookies because we are nice. We get cookies because Mrs. Wilson is nice."

Who Is the Lord That I Should Obey Him?

Some Christians have been like the self-assured Pharaoh who asked Moses, "Who is the Lord that I should obey His voice?" (Ex. 5:2). Directly or indirectly, many believers have asked a similar question: "Who is Jesus Christ that He should command total obedience from His people?" As a result, the awakening church is now looking around in despair, surveying the wreckage resulting from her ignorance of God's personhood, her lack of discipleship and partial obedience. Years of passivity and careless compromise have taken a great toll. For ages the church has talked about the price of obedience; now she is learning the dreadful price of disobedience.

Just a Glimpse of Him

I know people who are absolutely fanatical about our city's National Football League team, the Kansas City Chiefs. They know detailed information on every player; they keep up with every trade rumor and can recite the scheduled games backward. They meditate on it day and night. They press on to learn all they can about their beloved team.

Those who do not press on in pursuit of the breadth, length, height and depth of God will eventually become bored with their faith (Eph. 3:18). Their shallow understanding doesn't capture their imaginations, much less inflame their passions.

The great need of the church is to see, know and discover the indescribable glory of who God is. Seeing the heart, mind and character of God will cure our compromise and instability and motivate us to righteousness and holy passion. Personal, experiential knowledge of the person of Jesus will fuel obedience and zeal. It will put a stop to our restlessness and discontent. A new depth of intimacy with Him will extinguish our boredom and capture our hearts. Just a glimpse of Him....

John, whom Jesus surnamed "Son of Thunder" (Mark 3:17) because of his impetuous, stormy temperament, became one of the most prominent of the apostles. As he walked with Jesus, John's rashness, intolerance and selfish ambition were replaced by holy gentleness and passionate love.

John's own Gospel makes it clear that he was greatly beloved by the Lord. He was one of the three apostles who were closest to Jesus. He was allowed to witness the raising of Jairus's daughter (Matt. 9:18-19) and to be present at the transfiguration (Luke 9:28-36). It was John who reclined on Jesus' breast at the Passover feast (John 13:23). John was present at Christ's trial and was the only apostle who stood near the cross upon which Jesus was nailed. Just before the Lord died, it was to John, not to His own half-brothers and sisters, that Jesus entrusted the care of His mother Mary (John 19:26-27). It is this beloved friend of Jesus who writes in Revelation:

> I was in the Spirit on the Lord's day, and I heard behind me a loud voice like the sound of a trumpet..."I am the Alpha and the Omega...who is and who was and who is to come...." And having turned I saw...one like a son of man, clothed in a robe reaching to the feet, and girded across His breast with a golden girdle. And His head and His hair were white like white wool, like snow; and His eyes were like a flame of fire; and His feet were like burnished bronze, when it has been caused to glow in a furnace, and His voice was like the sound of many waters. And in His right hand He held seven stars; and out of His mouth came a sharp two-edged sword; and His face was like the sun shining in its strength (Rev. 1:10,8,12-16).

Think of it. The Living Bible says John was Christ's *closest friend* (John 13:23). But when the Lord, whom John had served faithfully, appeared to him in His awesome majesty and glory, John "fell at His feet as a dead man" (Rev. 1:17). Imagine a man of John's spiritual stature and experience being totally overcome by this brief glimpse of the beloved Friend he had served faithfully for more than sixty years.

When we are exposed to even a portion of His consuming glory, as John was, we will be motivated to live free from sin, die to selfishness and give ourselves passionately to the Lord. When we gaze upon His loveliness we will gladly die to those things that are not like Him.

John saw Jesus in His humility. He looked just like us — not very transcendent. Paul wrote to the Philippians that Jesus, who existed in the form of God, emptied Himself to the point that He was made in the likeness of men. He went on to say that now He is exalted to the extent that at the sight of Him every knee would bow and confess that He is Lord (Phil. 2:5-11).

Although no one knew Jesus more intimately than John while He was on earth, the revelation of His resurrected exaltation caused John to fall at His feet as a dead man.

While Jesus walked on earth, His glory was veiled in human flesh. Veils were used in the Bible to hide the glory of God. A veil was put over Moses' face to hide the glory, a veil hid the holy of holies and glory of God in the tabernacle, and the writer of Hebrews spoke of the "veil, that is, His flesh" (Heb. 10:20).

There is one other veil that Paul talked about in his letter to the Corinthians that also hides the glory of God. It is the veil that covers the heart and prevents a person from beholding the glory of Christ (2 Cor. 3:7-18).

The revelation of the true knowledge of the glorified Christ will transform you. Paul ends his discussion of the veil over the heart with this statement:

> But we all, with unveiled face beholding as in a mirror the glory of the Lord, are being transformed into the same image from glory to glory, just as from the Lord, the Spirit (2 Cor. 3:18).

The Irresistible Force

The enemy has assaulted the people of God. He has weakened and destroyed our foundation of the knowledge of

God. He has sought to defeat us by diluting our passion for Jesus and diverting us from our divine purpose. Satan has done his job well. But in His arsenal God has reserved the secret weapon of all the ages — the awesome knowledge of the splendor of the person of Jesus. The blazing light and majestic loveliness of the knowledge of God are about to shine into the community of the redeemed, and all the dark forces of hell will not be able to overpower it.

John wrote his account many years after the other three Gospel writers. As he looked back he commented on the irresistible nature of the knowledge of Jesus Christ.

> His life is the light that shines through the darkness — and the darkness can never extinguish it (John 1:5, TLB).

The splendor and glory of Jesus Christ will capture the affections of the church in a new way. Compromise and passivity will be solved as the Lord allows us to gaze upon Him with deeper insight into His personal beauty and glory. The body of Christ will rediscover Christ's personhood and majesty. When we do, we will give ourselves to Him in unparalleled affection and obedience.

FOUR

From Intimate Knowledge to Passionate Love

I walked into the little storefront room to speak to a group of new Christians, never dreaming that my life was about to be changed forever. I was twenty-one years old, eager to give everything I had to serve God who had shown me such unconditional love. As a young pastor, I had even foolishly determined that the best way for me to serve Him would be to remain single for the rest of my life!

My eyes scanned the little group of Christians who had gathered in the room. It was then I noticed the beautiful, young, blonde girl across the room. I flipped out! I had never felt such intense emotions as those that filled me as I gazed across the room at Diane, the girl who was to become my wife. On our first date I was amazed that she seemed to share my feelings, and we became engaged after just one date.

My deep love for Diane and my desire to be with her helped me understand the love Christ felt for His bride. His prayer in John 17 especially moved me: "Father, I desire that they also, whom Thou hast given Me, be with Me where I am" (John 17:24). Here was my Lord, only hours before His agonizing death at Calvary, crying out to the Father with intense cravings for His bride — for me!

He was consumed with love for His bride and longed to have His bride with Him for eternity.

I took a fresh look at this high priestly prayer, which is, I believe, the most significant intercessory prayer in all of Scripture.

Toward the end of the recorded prayer the focus changes from the first generation of Christians as Jesus begins to pray for the church throughout history. He intercedes for all future believers who will come to know Him. We find prophetic promises in these verses for the church. We see the purpose of God in a way that cannot be found in any other place in Scripture. Once you go beyond a casual, superficial reading of verses 20-26, you will find that every phrase contains several levels of meaning.

Jesus gave us a powerful promise: "I will build My church; and the gates of Hades shall not overpower it" (Matt. 16:18). And at the end of His great, prophetic prayer He gave us a glimpse of the powerful and passionate church He would build:

> And I have declared to them Your name, and will declare it, that the love with which You loved Me may be in them, and I in them (John 17:26, NKJV).

How magnificent it is to see the Son of God praying for the

church, His beloved bride, one last time while He is still clothed in human flesh. Christ's prayer for such a church will undoubtedly be answered. It was directed by the Father, energized by the Holy Spirit and prayed in accordance with the Father's will. Jesus never prayed amiss.

Obviously this prayer contains an eternal dimension, but verses 21-23 reveal that the answer to this prayer lies not just in heaven. It will come to pass on this side of eternity so the unsaved can witness it. Jesus prayed that the world would behold such a church. The beginnings of its fulfillment lie in this age.

The Four Prophetic Statements in the Priestly Prayer

And I have declared to them Your name,
And will declare it,
That the love with which You loved Me may be in
    them,
And I in them (John 17:26, NKJV).

In this verse we find four key phrases describing Christ's earthly ministry. Let's look at these phrases one at a time, examining them more closely.

1. "I Have Declared to Them Your Name"

"I have declared to them Your name." That was the consuming purpose beating in the heart of Jesus during His three and a half years of earthly ministry. When it was all over, He summed up His entire earthly ministry by saying to His Father, "I've made Your name known to them."

Jesus had given the people a revelation of the knowledge of God and let them know what His Father was like. He made known to them the splendor of His Father's glorious personality.

I don't think Jesus Christ enjoys anything more than revealing to others the infinite splendor, awesome beauty and eternal loveliness of His Father. Every aspect of His ministry reflects the indescribable loveliness of God the Father. Here, at the end of His life on earth, Jesus' great claim is that He has made the Father known.

We sometimes talk about the ministry of Jesus only in terms of physical and emotional healing or the preaching and teaching of the gospel. But the ministry of Jesus was not confined just to miracles and doctrine. Both of these categories of Christ's ministry support the greater element of His mission on this earth. The ministry of Jesus was most significantly defined by His reflection of the infinite glory and splendor of His Father.

When people heard Jesus' words, observed His lifestyle and beheld His perfectly balanced personality and flawless character, they received a glimpse of the splendor and beauty of what God the Father is like.

It was Christ's glory to reveal His Father, yet you and I have the same privilege and responsibility. Paul reminds us of that fact:

> But thanks be to God, who always leads us in His triumph in Christ, and manifests through us the sweet aroma of the knowledge of Him in every place (2 Cor. 2:14).

The Spirit of God leads us into triumph and victory so that we can manifest the sweet aroma of the knowledge of God everywhere we go. I experienced this triumph when I learned to release the anger and bitterness I had felt as a result of my brother's injury. As I let go of the anger, the Holy Spirit filled that spot with love and a new understanding of the heart of God. God desires that we experience fellowship with the Holy Spirit so that we will be transformed — led into victory from the inside out — a victory touching our hearts, minds and emotions. Then we will manifest the sweet fragrance of the knowledge of God in private, in public and in all our casual interactions. That's what Jesus did.

A sweet aroma is often the manifestation of the presence of God. When we see God in another person, whether in their actions, words or quiet spirits, a pure freshness touches our hearts. Every time the Spirit of God enables us to break a bondage or to triumph over an addiction or weakness and come into victory, that conquest releases in us more of the fragrance of a glorious person named Jehovah, God the Father (2 Cor. 2:14).

Jesus described His ministry as making His Father's name known to others. My goal is to help people think of ministry as more than something that happens in meetings or when we serve, counsel or pray for others. *Ministry* at its most basic definition is "the manifestation of the knowledge of God through our lives."

The invisible aroma of the knowledge of God that the apostle Paul talked about has power. It lifts us from one degree of life to another. Our hearts become softer. We grow more caring, compassionate, patient, loving and forgiving. We become more sensitive to the Spirit of God. We are more like Jesus. In order to grow into maturity, we must know God the Father more intimately. Our most vital ministry is revealing the beauty and splendor of God's personality to others.

It's easy to read a book or listen to a tape, memorizing new truths to talk about. It's easy to be an echo instead of a voice. But there is a certain quality of ministry that comes only as you and I touch God in reality in our secret lives.

To be mature Christians, each one of us must have a secret life in God hidden from the eyes of others. I remember the early days of becoming intimate with God. I would come before Him with a list of needs and wants. I struggled to feel His presence as I tossed my words into the air, never really experiencing the awesomeness of His presence with me.

I recall one particular time when I had isolated myself in

my office for a time of prayer. I had been studying the Song of Solomon and began praying the invitation of Jesus to set His seal upon my heart: "Set me as a seal upon thine heart, as a seal upon thine arm: for love is strong as death; jealousy is cruel as the grave: the coals thereof are coals of fire, which hath a most vehement flame" (Song 8:6, KJV). I became overwhelmed with God's presence. He was softening my heart at that moment. Tears flowed down my face.

Not wanting to lose the preciousness of the moment, I quietly buzzed my secretary and told her not to let anyone or anything interrupt me for the next thirty minutes. I became totally immersed in the presence of God.

I had been worshipping at His feet for about fifteen minutes when my secretary suddenly rang into my office.

"What are you doing?" I asked her with irritation. "I didn't want to be disturbed yet."

"I'm so sorry," she responded. "But you have a call, and the caller says it is very important that he speak to you right away."

Annoyed at being distracted from these intimate moments with God, I picked up the phone. An acquaintance of mine was on the other end of the line. "Mike," he began excitedly, "I had a dream about you last night. The Lord has very clearly impressed upon me that I am to give you a particular verse as His message to you."

My annoyance left as I listened to his words: "God says He has set you as a seal upon His heart, as a seal upon His arm. He wanted you to know that right now."

My awesome God loved me enough to respond to my yearnings the moment I voiced them to Him. Indeed, He had sent the answer on the way to me even as I entered into that secret time with Him.

As we commune with Him in prayer, meditate on His Word and behold His glory in the secret place, a beautiful and unique expression of Christ is developed in us.

A more mature ministry is birthed out of a greater prayer

life. It's more than having longer prayer times. It's possessing that quality of heart that responds to God in a greater way, a heart that yearns and reaches for Him, just as the face of a flower turns toward the sun.

The church desperately needs to recapture this focus of Christ's ministry. We, too, must seek to reveal the nature and splendor of the personality of God to His creation. Like Jesus, may you and I be able to say, "I have declared to them Your name."

2. *"And Will Declare It"*

In the next breath Jesus made a glorious statement pertaining to the future: "...and [I] will declare it [Your name]." But Jesus knew that even when He was seated at His Father's right hand, He would continue to reveal the majestic heart of the Father through the ministry of the Holy Spirit. One of His priorities would be to unveil and reveal the passions, desires and pleasures of the Father to His church.

Before Jesus comes *for* the church, He's going to come *to* the church — to people who know the Lord in the loveliness of His personality. We will all come "to the unity of the faith, and of the knowledge of the Son of God, to a mature man, to the measure of the stature which belongs to the fulness of Christ" (Eph. 4:13). His majestic splendor and indescribable loveliness will be revealed to His people. The name of God will be made known in the nations. The church will be filled with the intimate knowledge of God the Father, Son and Holy Spirit. Thus the church will be matured and perfected.

Christ's greatest passion is to continue to reveal the Father. That's what He is doing now in His heavenly ministry at the right hand of the Father. That is what He will be doing through all eternity. The church today must not be out of harmony with the present ministry of Jesus — revealing the Father to people's hearts. When others come in touch with the resurrected Jesus they will be captured by the loveliness, beauty and splendor of God's personality.

3. "...*That the Love With Which You Loved Me May Be in Them*"

"I have declared to them Your name, and will declare it." Why? "That the love with which You loved Me may be in them." When Jesus introduces us to the depths of His Father's heart we "see God" in a greater way. Seeing God awakens passionate love for Jesus. Seeing affects our feelings. Our emotions are changed when we see God's splendor.

Jesus is praying that the body of Christ will love Him the way the Father loves Him. That's a pretty awesome prayer. But Jesus is going to reveal the Father, and, in turn, the Father is going to capture our hearts for the Son. Jesus must be praying something like this:

> Father, You are so infinitely beautiful. Your splendor is beyond mankind's understanding. I want to make You known. I know You will capture the hearts of the people for Me. They will feel for Me as You feel for Me. My beloved bride, My eternal companion, My partner forever, the one You ordained to rule with Me as a co-heir, will love Me as You love Me.

Here we can see a significant dynamic at work within the Godhead. God the Father desires a people who are awakened in their affections and passions for Jesus. A people who see and feel what God sees and feels when He looks at His beloved Son. God is going to have *a passionate church* that loves Jesus as God loves Him.

The Father exercised infinite wisdom, power and goodness when He chose the Son's bride for Him and has ordained that she have extravagant passion for His Son.

Yes, the church will be filled with activities and ministries, but the single most distinctive issue in God's heart is to capture the church with passionate affections for His dear

Son. The Holy Spirit is zealous to accomplish that purpose in this hour.

In September 1985 our church had just started several new outreach programs. In the midst of these activities God spoke to three members of the leadership team, giving the same message to each: "You have overdone your emphasis on activities and ministries. You need to refocus on prayer and intercession."

We immediately gathered the church together, repented and regained our focus on intimacy. For several days we prayed every day, all day long. As our hearts were captured with love for God, the Holy Spirit poured out in an instant a glorious refreshing that permeated the prayer life of our church for several years to come.

In today's fast-lane living it's easy to allow our lives to blur out of focus and lose perspective with a full day at the office, activities every night of the week and household chores or a second job on the weekend. As William Wordsworth wrote almost two hundred years ago, "The world is too much with us...Getting and spending, we lay waste our powers."[1] In all of our getting, we must acquire passion for God.

Sometimes I become distracted from this mission. I was ministering during the summer of 1984 at various churches. After one particular service a man came up to me and offered to send me on an evangelistic trip to several different countries. It seemed to be a great opportunity for ministry, and I was thrilled at the prospect.

But when I returned home I wasn't so sure I should accept his offer. Our church was in the middle of an intense period of focusing on prayer, and somehow I felt as though I would be violating that emphasis by leaving.

As I sought the Lord for an answer, a friend called to give me counsel that he felt strongly about. In essence he said, "I know a large door has opened for you. But the Lord has called you to be singleminded in the prayer room during this season — He wants you to give Him undistracted devotion."

Instantly, this verse came to mind: "But I fear, lest by any means, as the serpent beguiled Eve through his subtlety, so your minds should be corrupted from the simplicity that is in Christ" (2 Cor. 11:3, KJV). I knew I had my answer — I did not go on the trip.

I have to remind myself that I am not called to be a spiritual politician. I am called to be a man filled with holy passion and extravagant affection for Jesus. That is what I want to minister to people. That is what I have chosen to make the determining purpose of my life: knowing the Father's name and making it known, loving Jesus as the Father loves Him and inspiring others into intimacy with Him.

4. "...And I in Them"

First, Christ says, "I have declared to them Your name." Then He says, "I will declare it." Why? So that the same love the Father has for Jesus would fill and energize the hearts of all those who believe in Him. Now Jesus states the fourth principle, "I will be in them."

As the riches of the knowledge of God are revealed, what is the result? The quality of love the Father has for the Son will be in the church. Jesus will dwell in His people, manifesting His overflowing life through them.

The cycle goes all the way around. When Jesus manifests His life's ministry through us, we declare God's name and make Him known to others. Then they, in turn, are awakened with passion when they see God, and they fall in love with Him.

Every prayer of Jesus was a prophetic promise. Every time He prayed it was according to the will of His Father. This prayer of Jesus Christ in John 17 will be answered. It's a wonderful, prophetic promise for the church!

A Revival of Intimacy and Passion

It takes the power of God to make God known. It takes the

knowledge of God to enable mankind to love God. It takes God to love God, and it takes God to know God.

The church is going to be filled with the knowledge of God. Jesus said it, and He's not going to fail. The Holy Spirit will use the release of this knowledge to awaken a sense of deep urgency for intimacy with Jesus. A revival of the intimate knowledge of God is coming, and as a result the church will be filled with holy passion for His Son. Divinely inspired intimacy and passion are on the Holy Spirit's agenda because they are prayers of Jesus.

Obviously, this prophetic prayer for the church has never been fulfilled. It is sadly apparent that today's church does not love Jesus as the Father does. Furthermore, we can find no place in history where that prayer has been fulfilled in any major worldwide way. But the Father Himself is committed to answering this prayer. The name of the Lord will be known intimately by His people, and the church will love Jesus as God the Father loves His Son, Jesus.

How Shall These Things Be?

Sometimes I've looked at the lukewarm, compromising church of our day and wondered, How shall these things be? How can such a glorious thing ever come to pass? But then I remember Israel's pathetic spiritual condition during the time of Christ's earthly ministry. Just like us, the nation of Israel and the world of that day didn't have a chance except that God was, is and ever shall be rich in mercy. At His appointed time, of His own will and out of His own good pleasure, God supernaturally intervened. The same flaming zeal in the heart of God that compelled Him to send Jesus the first time will accomplish His divine purposes in a compromising generation and a complacent and passionless church. The zeal of the Lord of hosts shall perform it.

It won't happen because we are better than other people. The source of passionate affections for Jesus will not be in us. Such passion always comes from seeing God's glorious personality and His work on the cross. It comes from encountering even just a brief, dim glimpse of who God is and what He did.

There is nothing Jesus wants more than a bride who loves what He loves and does what He does forever. He longs for a bride who will participate in the passions and purposes of His heart. Jesus Christ is going to have an eternal companion filled with holy, passionate affections for Him. Oh, how I want to be a part of a glorious, spotless church in our generation — a church filled with the knowledge of God, reflecting His glory and consumed with passion for Jesus. Such a church will be prepared to engage in the great conflict that is to come.

FIVE

"Kiss the Son
Lest He Be Angry"

Have you ever yearned to look into the days ahead and see what lies in store for the church? Would you like to understand exactly what's going on behind much of the chaos and upheaval in the world today?

In my travels in other countries, my heart has been broken over the growing immorality that I've witnessed. I am appalled by the nudity in public parks and the sinful activities that are so rampant in some of the major cities of our world. Evil and immorality have reached an all-time high. The world is consumed with the passions of sin. But it is a counterfeit passion. Many European nations can hope to be healed from the trauma of sin only as the church allows God to replace the counterfeit passion of the world with the pure, awesome passion of the Father for His people. We overcome sinful passions when God replaces them with holy passions.

Psalm 2 gives a better explanation of the current international conflicts than the headlines in today's newspapers. Take a moment to read these twelve verses now. Because this famous messianic psalm gives a prophetic description of end-times events, its greatest fulfillment lies in the days ahead. It reveals the rebellion of human leaders against God and His Word. This rebellion has escalated through history. It will culminate at the end of the age in the great conflict between God and Satan to establish who will rule the passions of the human heart.

A Divine Drama

Charles Haddon Spurgeon, the famous British preacher, described Psalm 2 in terms of a great, four-act drama.[1] The curtain goes up, and in the action of the first three verses the rebellious kings and rulers of the earth act out their parts in history. Then the curtain closes. The second act opens with God the Father at center stage responding to the evil leaders. The curtain closes and opens again for the third act. This time the Son of God has the starring role. King David takes the stage in the last act and sounds a warning that echoes down the corridors of time — from David's day to the second coming of the Lord.

The plot of the drama centers around the unified rebellion of the kings and rulers of the earth against God's sovereign decree that He will give all the nations and ends of the earth to His Son as His inheritance.

Shhhh! It's time to take our seats. The play is about to begin.

Act One: Satan's Agenda

As the curtain rises, the nations are in an uproar, and the rebellious kings and rulers of the earth are taking counsel together, plotting their strategy:

> Why do the nations rage,
> And the people plot a vain thing?
> The kings of the earth set themselves,
> And the rulers take counsel together,
> Against the Lord and against His Anointed, saying,
> "Let us break Their bonds in pieces
> And cast away Their cords from us" (vv. 1-3,
>   NKJV).

The kings of the earth are challenging God's right to command their obedience and to give Jesus the affections of the human race as His possession (v. 8).

Nothing in all creation is more significant to God than the soul of a human being. It is the seat of affections where love and true worship flow. Who and what will possess people's affections are of grave concern to the Father. We were made in His own image and likeness, fashioned and uniquely designed for His holy purposes. God would not send His beloved Son to die for anything in all creation except priceless, eternal human souls.

God designed the human soul to be passionate, abandoned and committed. That is the way the soul functions best. It sinks into restlessness, boredom, passivity and frustration if it has nothing worthy of giving itself to or sacrificing itself for. In other words, if we have nothing to die for, then we really have nothing to live for. God intended our souls to be captured, consumed and enthralled with Jesus. Our highest development and greatest fulfillment lie in worshipping Him and serving Him with an abandonment that will sacrifice everything.

As an inheritance, God the Father has promised the Son a

church filled with believers whose spirits are ablaze with affections and adoration for Jesus. The Father will never insult or sadden His beloved Son by presenting Him a church (the bride of Christ) that is bored, passive and compromising.

Passionless Christianity, so common today, is no threat to the devil. Focused on concepts and activities to the neglect of heartfelt affection and obedience to God, it brings no pleasure to God's heart. It doesn't even bring pleasure to the believer. But true Christianity sparks a flame in the human spirit. It ignites the heart with holy fervency for Jesus.

Satan, aware of God's agenda to capture human affections and consume them with passion for His Son, has devised an agenda of his own. To carry out his plans, Satan raises up his own passionate people, radically committed to one of the many forms of humanism, spiritualism and false religion. The source of their utter abandonment is hate, anger, pain, ambition or greed — not love for God.

Inspired by Satan, these wicked leaders violently oppose the idea of a passionate people consumed with affection for God's Son. They are committed unreservedly to raising up a corresponding passionate resistance against the holy things of God, which will eventually become a hellish rage against Jesus, coming to a red hot boil in the generation for which the Lord returns.

This raging conflict will be fought on many different battlegrounds: religious, social and political ideologies; the economy; science and medicine; morals and ethics; education, music and art.

Mark it: If an issue is important to man, you'll find Satan's fingerprints all over it. He always seeks to twist and pervert the issue to serve his interests. At his appointed time, rebellious, red hot passion will develop around that issue.

At the moment he may be promoting homosexuality, abortion, sex education which fosters an ungodly lifestyle, pornography or other sin issues. But Satan's real, underlying motive goes far beyond that issue. His desire is to capture the passions of the human race, because that is the highest priority on God's agenda.

Satan doesn't intend his perversion of human hearts to stop with the tremendous influx of indecency and immorality gripping the nations. He wants to push this thing way past mere immorality and indecency. His goal is for the nations of this earth to erupt with boiling rage against God. He is after militant, unified, passionate revolt against God's laws and even against His right to reign.

If you keep an eye on the spiritual temperature of national and international events, you will see the thermometer climbing higher and higher. Look at the United States, Europe and the Western world. Pockets of anger and rebellion are smoldering among those who influence and determine the general course of morality. Satan and his cohorts are fanning and feeding those flames so they will explode in rage and reckless revolt.

Make no mistake about it: First, he deceives the rulers and leaders. Then he unites them around his diabolical purposes. He teaches them how to devise clever ploys to capture public opinion and undermine righteousness. He provokes them to overthrow the edicts of God and cast off the restraints of God's written Word. They plot to erase the wise boundaries of right and wrong, good and evil that God has marked out in His Word for the human soul.

These deceived rulers take their stand firmly before God, challenging His right to give His Son this inheritance.

> "The kingdoms of this world belong to us!" they rage. "Who is He that the world should give *Him* passionate affection? The passions of mankind belong to the kings and leaders of the earth! We — not Your Son — have the right to the affections of men!"

The momentum of unholy passion builds. Foolish, dark-minded rulers from every level and arena of society — lawmakers, educators, entertainers, advertisers, corporate heads, religious leaders, media moguls and others plot to attack the holy commandments and precepts of God. They seek first to dilute, then to demolish them from society, one by one.

> "We will not obey You!" they sneer. "We will break Your Word in pieces and cast away Your commandments. Right and wrong are only what we decide. We will live and do as we please. We will live for our own pleasure and not Yours. We will not worship You; we will worship mankind. The Son has no inheritance in the hearts and nations of this earth!"

As the angry shouts and jeers of the wicked grow louder, the curtain falls on act 1.

Act 2: God's Agenda

As act 2 opens, God is seated upon His throne in the heavens, mocking the rebellious kings of the earth and laughing at their vain schemes and foolish plots.

> He who sits in the heavens shall laugh;
> The Lord shall hold them in derision.
> Then He shall speak to them in His wrath,
> And distress them in His deep displeasure:
> "Yet have I set My King
> On My holy hill of Zion" (vv. 4-6, NKJV).

Spurgeon said this scoffing, mocking laugh of God at the wicked kings of the earth is the most terrible, terrifying laugh one could imagine.[2]

These foolish kings have planned it all out. They think they own the money of the earth. They think they hold the power. They make their own laws. They control the world's systems and institutions. Science and technology have become tools to serve their wicked, selfish purposes. Therefore, the rebellious rulers think that if they work together in total unity, they can actually overrule God's purposes for planet Earth.

But God laughs at them, for He knows that their success has been only what He has granted them. The nations are as a drop in a bucket to Him. A mere speck of dust on the scales of time. The nations of the world have no ability to resist His edicts. He can bring them down with a flick of His finger. He can blow them away with the faintest breath from His mouth.

> "I have news for you," says the Father. "I have *already* appointed My King on His holy hill. It has been established forever in the eternal counsels of the Godhead. The inheritance of My Son is sure. People of all ages, races, languages and nations will be filled with holy passion for My Son. He will have a passionate church whose affections are totally filled with Him. The zeal of the Lord of hosts shall bring it to pass."

Revealing what is soon to come, act 2 closes as the battle lines are drawn. The people of the earth, now radically abandoned to one of two clear-cut agendas, take their places on one side or the other.

Act 3: The Son Claims His Inheritance

Standing in center stage as the curtain rises is the anointed One, Jesus Christ. The narrator proclaims loudly:

> I will declare the decree:
> The Lord has said to Me,
> "You are My Son,
> Today I have begotten You.
> Ask of Me, and I will give You
> The nations for Your inheritance,

> And the ends of the earth for Your possession.
> You shall break them with a rod of iron;
> You shall dash them in pieces like a potter's ves-
>   sel" (vv. 7-9, NKJV).

In this decree we see that the Bible is not just about God's plans and provision for mankind. It is also about God's plans and provision for His Son. Scripture describes a twofold inheritance: One part focuses on man, while the other focuses on God. We have an inheritance in which *our* delight and fulfillment are fundamental. God has an inheritance in which *His* delight is fundamental. The church must teach this twofold inheritance. We must be committed both to delight in and to give delight to God. The inheritance for us, the people of God, is the ability to experience both the blessings and the love of a passionate God. The inheritance for God is a passionate people. But He will experience His inheritance only as we become radically committed to Him. We must seek to experience revival that emphasizes both of these truths together.

The Father invites Jesus into a place of intercession:

> Ask of Me, and I will give You
> The nations for Your inheritance,
> And the ends of the earth for Your possession (v.
>   8, NKJV).

In the final hours before His crucifixion, Jesus engaged in that intercession, praying for all believers (see John 17). And at this moment He is still interceding in heaven for His own (see Heb. 7:25).

The Son's throne is forever and ever, and the scepter of His kingdom is one of absolute righteousness. He begins His rule with kindness, for it is the kindness of God that leads mankind to repentance (Rom. 2:4). But if kindness does not work, and if mankind refuses to yield to the awakening, wooing influences of God's grace, Christ Jesus will rule them by force through His terrifying judgments. His iron scepter will dash the rebellious to pieces, shattering them effortlessly like pottery.

What eternal riches God has offered mankind. What dignity and destiny He has bestowed upon the human race by designing us to live eternally for the praise of His glory. What a privilege to become the passion and pleasure of Christ Jesus. There are dimensions of pleasure and fulfillment that can never be experienced until we say a passionate, abandoned yes to the Lordship of Jesus Christ. Yet so few believers have really said that yes to God.

It is little wonder that the unbelieving world looks at a bored, compromising, bickering church and sneers, "If that's what a Christian is, forget it." The most powerful witness you and I can give sinners is a radiant life demonstrating that the will of God is good, acceptable and perfect. Nonbelievers are looking for a contented, fulfilled people who aren't trying to cast off God's restraints — a people who are joyfully abandoned and totally committed to His cause. They long for something or someone that's worth being passionate for — something that costs them everything. But people have already discovered no cause or person is worthy of their total commitment here. Causes have crumbled into decay and deceptive rubble, and heroes have fallen from their pedestals. They need to see Christians who have taken up their crosses, turned their backs to the world and given their all to the Christ who gave everything to them.

Act 4: The Psalmist's Solemn Warning

The curtain rises, and King David steps forward to enact the last scene of the drama. He issues a solemn threefold warning to all who are foolish enough to believe they can challenge God and prevail.

Now therefore, be wise, O kings;
Be instructed, you judges of the earth.

Serve the Lord with fear,
And rejoice with trembling.
Kiss the Son, lest He be angry,
And you perish in the way,
When His wrath is kindled but a little.
Blessed are all those who put their trust in Him
   (vv. 10-12, NKJV).

"Serve the Lord with fear, and rejoice with trembling. Kiss the Son, lest He be angry," warns David.

God is awesome in splendor and terrifying in His greatness. This royal One has no superior — no equal. When we get a glimpse of His eternal, majestic splendor and beauty we are filled with reverential fear. We tremble before Him.

If we feel only fear and trembling in the presence of God, we will never experience the fullness of His grace. David says we are to rejoice before Him as well. We are to exult and rejoice in the benefits of our inheritance.

But there is yet another dimension. "Kiss the Son," says David, speaking symbolically of our affections being filled with passion for Jesus. There is to be an intimate, affectionate, passionate dimension in our relationship with Him.

Some churches emphasize awe and trembling. Historically, holiness-type churches have focused on the greatness of God, often leaving little room for rejoicing and affectionate worship.

Others concentrate on rejoicing and blessing. Some of today's charismatic churches have focused on the authority of the believer and the privileges we have in Christ — to the exclusion of His awesome majesty and judgment.

Still others are committed to affectionate intimacy with God with a passionate response of love toward Jesus. But God has fashioned the human spirit in such a way that we need all three dimensions — trembling, rejoicing and kissing — in our relationship with Him. We need to ask the Holy Spirit to revive in our own hearts, as well as in the church, all three dimensions of the grace of God.

How about you? Are you committed to one dimension, but not to the other two? Are two of these dimensions developing in your relationship with Him, but not the third?

Maybe you've only seen a God who judges the rebellious. Maybe you walk before the Lord in faithfulness and reverential fear. You're good at trembling, but you've never seen a God in whom you can rejoice.

Perhaps you've never known a dimension of intimacy and affection, and the thought of kissing Christ is a little uncomfortable to you. But this is only symbolic language and not to be interpreted literally. It refers to our souls being stirred by Jesus. God longs to open our spirits so we can share in this great, divine exchange of soul-ravishing love.

When I first read verse 12 of Psalm 2, I was troubled. I didn't realize that the verse spoke symbolically of heart adoration. But because God dealt tenderly with me concerning my repeated failures, I understood. And my heart yearned to express my adoration for God.

The Lord wants to intertwine these three dimensions in you. He wants to bring them forth by His Holy Spirit. This threefold response of trembling, rejoicing and kissing is what comprises the inheritance promised to Jesus by the Father.

Finally, King David issues a warning to all who would be foolish enough to defy God: "Kiss the Son, lest He be angry, and you perish in the way, when His wrath is kindled but a little" (Ps. 2:12, NKJV).

Remember that the shepherd boy who stood with holy confidence before Goliath while King Saul and the army of Israel cowered in the background is the author of this psalm (see 1 Sam. 17). He is the young man whose heart was provoked with fiery indignation when the giant Philistine raised his fist and taunted the army of the living God. This fearless shepherd was so intimately acquainted with God's personality that he may have felt in his spirit the mocking laugh of God against Goliath's claims to defeat the God of Israel.

David's holy indignation had already enabled him to conquer the lion and bear in his private life, equipping him with experience and confidence to challenge Goliath and the powers of darkness Goliath represented. After all, he could not defeat the enemies in others if those same enemies still triumphed over him.

Refusing to wear the cumbersome religious armor of his day, David charged out to face Goliath. He didn't see *big* Goliath and *little* David as he ran toward the battle line. He didn't see a huge sword and a little sling shot. All he saw were the powers of darkness mocking and defying the living God. David's stone and sling were irrelevant. He had the name of the Lord of hosts and the unshakeable confidence that His God would prevail!

The Coming Conflict

Once more the lines of battle are being drawn. Who will control the affections of the human race? Satan will have his taunting Goliaths with their spears and swords. God will have His end-times army of Davids who are filled with the knowledge of their almighty God. They will not draw back from the fight, for they fear neither death nor defeat. Their captain is the Lord of hosts, and He has never lost a battle.

Christ shall have His inheritance. Goliath's taunting jeers will be silenced. The last sounds the wicked giant hears before his massive head rolls in the dust will be the whistling of a tiny stone...and God's terrifying laugh.

SIX

Strongholds
of the Mind

I was twenty-three years old and pastoring a church in St. Louis in 1978 when Luke, my first son, was born. The day after Luke's birth I had appointments I simply could not cancel. By the time the last appointment rolled around, I was aching so badly to see my one-day-old son, I couldn't even listen to the person talking to me.

Finally I broke away, jumped into my car and went speeding down the road to see that little guy named Luke. I had this incredible ache, this unbelievable longing and urgency to be with my new son, to look into his face.

Suddenly an overwhelming realization hit my heart, and I

found myself asking, "You mean, God, that the way I feel about my little Lukey is the way You feel about me?"

An urgent question came to my mind: "How much do you love your son?"

"Oh, Lord," I actually responded aloud, "I would give everything to this boy — everything!"

Then this Scripture verse seemed to explode in my heart:

> If you then, being evil, know how to give good gifts to your children, how much more shall your Father who is in heaven give what is good to those who ask Him! (Matt. 7:11).

The realization of the depth and magnitude of God's love for me was so emotionally overpowering, I pulled off the road and wept.

Many of the problems in the body of Christ today are merely the result of a more fundamental problem at the very heart of the church. Our generation is paying a heavy price for the decline of the intimate knowledge of God. It is evident as we count the number of spiritual leaders who have fallen; as we read about the repeated financial scandals in the church; and as church after church experiences disappointment, bitterness and hostility among its members.

This woeful decline has brought about the secularizing of our churches and the decay of our inner lives, resulting in boredom, passivity and compromise. A. W. Tozer placed his finger squarely on the problem when he wrote:

> A condition...has existed in the church for some years and is steadily growing worse. I refer to the loss of the concept of majesty from the popular religious mind. The church has surrendered her once lofty concept of God and has substituted for it one so low, so ignoble, as to be utterly unworthy of thinking, worshipping men. This she has done not

deliberately, but little by little and without her knowledge; and her very unawareness only makes her situation all the more tragic. The low view of God entertained almost universally among Christians is the cause of a hundred lesser evils everywhere among us.[1]

Christianity in America and much of the world right now is not God-centered. It's centered on needs, success, wholeness or spiritual gifts. Although all these issues are important, they are not to be the focus, but the by-product, of genuine spirituality. Emotional, spiritual and physical blessings are the overflow from God-centered Christianity, not the fountainhead.

The church, having neglected her diligent pursuit of the intimate knowledge of God, has lost her joy and affection and the consciousness of His divine presence. She has lost her spirit of worship and her sense of awe and adoration. She has replaced truth with activity and substituted religious rituals for heartfelt relationship.

A God in Our Image

We have taken God for granted. We have allowed materialism, secularism and the love of things to smother the flame of God in our souls. We have created God in our own image, an image that is erroneous and tragically inadequate. Many in our generation have made for themselves a God they can use and control — a "heavenly butler" who waits on them hand and foot, catering to their every whim. Others have fashioned a jovial, one-of-the-guys kind of God who understands mankind's necessity to lie or cheat or indulge in a harmless little sexual diversion now and then.

To some believers, God is warm, approachable and forgiving. To others, He is cold, aloof and condemning. Regardless of how we see Him, what you and I think about God is the most important thing about us. We will eventually be shaped by the image of God we carry in our minds.

Individuals often come to me with inaccurate, inadequate concepts of God's love and forgiveness. I may explain over and over, "God loves you, and He has forgiven you," but the believer responds, "I don't feel as if He loves me. I feel as if God has a big hammer in His hand, and He's just waiting to find a good enough reason to hit me over the head."

I may counsel and pray with the person time and time again, ministering the love and forgiveness of God, only to hear the individual say, "I wish I could believe that God is the way you say He is. I want to believe He really loves me, but I just can't grasp it."

Do you see how that person's life is being shaped by his or her inadequate concepts of God? As long as the individual continues to believe these or other lies about God and His nature, he or she will never mature into a strong Christian. That person will live in fear, insecurity and defeat. Sooner or later, those fears and insecurities will bear poisonous fruit in the individual's own life and relationships with others.

I know it did in my own life. In the early years of my ministry I was hesitant and afraid to minister to others if I was going through a period of personal failure or temptation. I didn't want to pray for people — I didn't think my prayers would help them.

I compared my experience to the days when I played college football. If I had had several bad days of practice, the coach didn't let me play in the game that week. I thought God was like that: Either I did great in practice, in my personal spiritual life, or I wasn't good enough to participate in ministry.

Today I am often amazed at how God uses me in ministry at those times when I feel most inadequate spiritually. But I've learned that God's strength is still present in my weakness.

Satan goes to great lengths to distort our concepts of God. But because such distortions can serve the enemy's "interests" in our lives, he is willing to invest as much time and work as it takes to secure those vulnerable areas of our minds for his own purposes.

We dare not decide to ignore and just learn to live with the lies and misconceptions about God's personality that have been planted there. Those inaccurate, inadequate concepts place us in great peril. To the degree that our ideas about God are lower than the truth of God, to that degree we are surely weakened and defeated. In those places and upon the foundation of distorted truth, Satan is able to gain ground and set up his strongholds in our lives.

Strongholds of the Mind

For the weapons of our warfare are not of the flesh, but divinely powerful for the destruction of fortresses. We are destroying speculations and every lofty thing raised up against the knowledge of God, and we are taking every thought captive to the obedience of Christ (2 Cor. 10:4-5).

What exactly does Paul mean by a stronghold? In ancient times a stronghold was a fortress built with walls and defenses to provide protection against the enemy. The fortress King Saul had in Gibeah, about four miles north of Jerusalem, is a good example. The two-story structure with corner towers had a six-feet-thick outer wall surrounded by a sloping bank of earth which forced attackers to climb uphill to reach the fortress.[2]

Other strongholds were fortified dens and caves high on ridges or mountainsides that were difficult to assault (see Judg. 6:2; 1 Sam. 23:14,19). Towns and cities, strengthened and carefully prepared against enemy attack, were also sometimes referred to as strongholds. The Scriptures record that even before the Israelites entered Canaan, they were terrified by the reports of cities "great and fortified up to heaven" (Num. 13:28; Deut. 1:28).

As the early Christians read the apostle Paul's letters they would be familiar with the psalms that referred to God as a stronghold — a fortress or refuge for His people (see Ps. 9:9; 59:9,17).

It's not surprising that Paul, when teaching about the believer's warfare with Satan and his demonic legions, drew upon the familiar term *stronghold*. Paul uses the term to describe any type of thinking that exalts itself above the knowledge of God, giving the enemy a protected place of influence in a person's thought life.

A spiritual fortress made of thoughts can be a fortified dwelling place where demonic forces can hide. From that stronghold they defend themselves and protect Satan's interests and investments in that person.

A stronghold in the mind is a collection of thoughts in agreement with Satan — thoughts that are lies against what God has revealed about Himself.

Wrong concepts and ideas about God are not automatically eliminated when we are born again. Paul instructs the believers in Colossae to "put on the new self who is *being renewed* to a true knowledge according to the image of the One who created him" (Col. 3:10, italics added).

We are continually in the process of being renewed by a true knowledge according to the personality and likeness of God. Until we are walking in that full, perfect knowledge of God, you and I must not make the mistake of assuming that the process of change is over.

Exposing Satan's Strongholds

Jesus made a statement about Himself with regard to Satan that sheds light on the idea of the enemy's having certain interests and investments in our lives. "I will not speak much more with you, for the ruler of the world is coming, and he has nothing in Me" (John 14:30).

Jesus had no sin, no erroneous thinking processes, no

wrong attitudes, no impure motives or careless habits. Satan could find *nothing* in Jesus — not even one square inch of territory — to which he could lay claim.

The enemy is continually seeking occasions where he can obtain a foothold in our lives, areas of spiritual darkness which he can rightfully claim. Sin and spiritual ignorance invite his attack. As a shark is drawn to blood, so the devil is drawn to darkness.

When I speak of areas of spiritual darkness, I'm referring not to a random sinful action here and there, but to an area where truth has been usurped by a lie.

As Paul explained to the Corinthians, this darkness is like a veil that hinders and obscures the illuminating, liberating light of the gospel in the minds of unbelievers.

> That they might not see the light of the gospel of the glory of Christ, who is the image of God (2 Cor. 4:4).

Here Paul tells us what the light is. The light is the understanding of the gospel of the glory of Christ. In other words, understanding the glory of Christ includes understanding who He is in His personality and what He did in His redemptive work on the cross.

> For God, who said, "Light shall shine out of darkness," is the One who has shone in our hearts to give the light of the knowledge of the glory of God in the face of Christ (2 Cor. 4:6).

What is the light of the gospel? It is the knowledge of the glory of God, as manifested and revealed in Jesus' personality and His work on the cross.

Satan's goal is to keep us in darkness. His strategy is to distort or restrict our knowledge of God so that it is erroneous and inadequate. Thus we are weakened and held in bondage. Satan does not want the light of the intimate knowledge of God to invade areas of moral and spiritual darkness. Therefore, in our hearts and minds he lays claim to every area of spiritual darkness he can find: sinful habits; areas of rebellion toward God; our unregenerate ideas, opinions and thought systems; carnal, spiritually immature ways of thinking; sympathetic thoughts toward sin; and self-excusing rationalizations. Then he utilizes these to erect *strongholds* in order to protect his investments and interests.

Learning More About Strongholds

As a young Christian I was driven to achieve spiritually, emotionally and physically. When I failed I became angry. When I succeeded I became proud. Eventually I recognized that, like the Pharisees of old, I was trying to earn God's favor and becoming legalistic.

How does the enemy construct a spiritual stronghold in your life? First, he starts with a foundation of lies and half-truths. Usually these are lies about the personality of God or about how God views you as a person in Christ. Then up go thick walls, brick by brick: vain philosophies, erroneous interpretations of Scripture, inaccurate ideas about the person of God, and distorted perceptions of how God sees and feels about you when, in your spiritual immaturity, you sin. Held together by the mortar of mistaken reasoning, the walls rise higher and higher. Soon lofty towers of stubborn pride and vain imaginations loom above the shadows.

Satan erects every stronghold he can to keep us from the true knowledge of God. To the degree he is successful, we will not enjoy an intimate relationship with the Lord. We will not come to know for ourselves the loveliness and excellence of God's personality. The result is that our emotional lives will not be released into full affection for God.

Breaking Strongholds Through
the True Knowledge of God

We must adopt an offensive posture if we are to break free from a stronghold. If believers are ever to be truly free, they must first know the truth about the personality of God and how He views us in Christ. As Jesus tells us in John 8:32, "And you shall know the truth, and the truth shall make you free."

Second, they must pursue an intimate relationship with God, who is a real person. They must hunger for Him and long to know Him intimately, searching for the true knowledge of God's personality as they look back over their shoulders at temptation and say no. It's by knowing the truth, then pursuing a person (God), along with resisting unholy passions and temptations, that Christians can walk in victory.

Our strong-willed determination to overcome our weaknesses and addictions is not our sanctification. Our sanctification is found in a *person:* Jesus Christ! *He Himself* "became to us wisdom from God, and righteousness and sanctification, and redemption" (1 Cor. 1:30).

When believers today are given just a little glimpse of the truth about Christ's awesome beauty and splendor, we — just like the people in the Bible who were granted similar insight — will be subdued. We will bow before Him in awe, and with gladness and affection we will abandon ourselves to Him.

Understanding God's Love for Us

Most Christians have vague, contradictory ideas about God's personality. And our ideas usually come from our relationships with earthly authority figures. If we think of the authority figures who were the most influential in our early years, we will find that many of our ideas of God are connected to these people.

Usually the most significant person in the forming of these ideas is one's earthly father. Also important are mothers or perhaps an athletic coach, a schoolteacher, a tutor or even a piano teacher — anyone who is looked up to and admired.

Our experience with these authority figures affects us emotionally. The following descriptions of earthly fathers may show how some of us have formed our ideas of God.

The Distant or Passive Father

The emotionally distant or passive father expresses his affections in a minimal way. He assumes you know he loves you, but he rarely speaks it. However, you don't know he sees or feels your pain or joy. When something wonderful or tragic happens, the passive father just nods his head. You begin to believe God is like that as well. He does not feel your pain or share your joy. He has little affections to express to you. You may reap strong emotional consequences if you are raised by this kind of father.

The Authoritarian Father

The authoritarian father intervenes to stop what you are doing. He hands out a list of dos and don'ts. He interrupts you and says no to the things that are important to you. Your heart is quenched by this. This kind of father does not honor your individuality. He is not interested in your desires or goals — only his own. He wants no partnership or deep intimacy with you, but only to be obeyed.

The Abusive Father

Abusive fathers inflict pain on their children deliberately, hurting them emotionally, mentally, physically and some-times sexually. There is no greater torment in life than the torment at the hands of an abusive father. It not only de-stroys the child's natural emotions, but it deeply shapes his relationship with God.

The Absent Father

The fourth type of father is one who is totally absent. Maybe he is the father you never knew, perhaps even dying before you were born. He is not like the passive father who is there yet does not communicate. He simply is never there. Therefore he never intervenes to help you in times of trouble. You feel totally abandoned and neglected by your earthly father. This hinders your ability to experience the presence of your heavenly Father.

The Accusing Father

The fifth father is the most common example. He is the accusing father. He proclaims to love you with his whole heart, but he judges you continually at every failure. In his mind he is trying to motivate you to do right. He thinks if he points our your failures, you will be motivated to try harder next time. He rarely shows you affection or affirms you. If you grew up with this type of father, you will have great difficulty understanding the love of your heavenly Father because you will think God is always accusing you.

This presents a dilemma for us, for God is not like our earthly authority figures. In Psalm 50:21 we read that God said, "You thought that I was altogether like you" (NKJV). But, " 'My thoughts are not your thoughts, nor are your ways My ways,' says the Lord. 'For as the heavens are higher than the earth, so are My ways higher than your ways' " (Is. 55:9, NKJV).

As high as the heavens are above the earth, so God's affections and emotions are higher than man's. The greatest father on the earth falls infinitely short of the emotions of God. There is no adequate human model to give a picture of God's heart.

You may think that it's easy for me to break strongholds through the true knowledge of God. After all, I had a lot of great examples who showed me what God is really like. I had an affectionate father who constantly encouraged and affirmed me; the Catholic priest who demonstrated commitment by teaching me for a year; that Christian high school coach who faithfully pursued me for God and invested his time in me; and those two youth pastors from the Presbyterian church who discipled me.

But what if my life had been different? What if I hadn't had a single positive force in my life to show me even a tiny glimmer of what God is really like? What if my father had hated me and constantly ridiculed me? What if he had molested me? What if he had beaten me until my spirit felt as bruised and bloody as my body? What if he had been a junkie, an alcoholic or an ex-con instead of a man everyone liked and respected?

What if all the other influences were negative? Then what would I think about God?

When I was introduced by the Holy Spirit to a smiling God, it changed my entire life. When I began to look up and think of a God with a big grin on His face when He looked at me, I imagined Him saying, "Oh, I love you. I have so much enjoyment in you — you fill Me with such pleasure."

I looked at myself and responded, "Who, me? Do You have the right person? Don't You see my sin and failure? How can You enjoy me when I have such weaknesses?"

But the Father lovingly answered, "I see the sincerity in your heart. You look at the outward man, but I see the cry in your heart to please Me. I feel great delight and pleasure over you!"

As I recognized this God with a big grin on His face when He looked at me, I realized I had an entirely wrong idea of what His personality was like. I saw that He wanted me to run *to* Him, not *away* from Him.

I've been a pastor for eighteen years. Through those years I have grieved and interceded for many individuals who have come to me with stories that were enough to make the angels weep — stories of molestation, abuse and perversion at the hands of cruel, selfish human beings. But even if those precious individuals had never known a single person who showed them real love, I know that God's Word offers each one bondage-breaking truth and joyful hope. And I have been able to share that truth and hope with them through personal counseling times.

The true knowledge of God's pure, faithful, passionate affections for you and me is far more powerful and life-transforming than any human witness we may or may not have had. It is the Holy Spirit, not human witnesses, who reveals God's love for us and makes Him real to our hearts, *and that revelation is available to everyone.*

People with wounded, broken spirits or perfectionist, performance-driven personalities often experience difficulty receiving from God. Sometimes we become so caught up in our own pressures, pain or anger that we don't even recognize His voice. But as we surrender our souls humbly to God, and our hearts begin crying out for the true, intimate knowledge of Him, He will answer. The Holy Spirit will open the Word of God to us, giving us understanding and teaching us to apply its truths to specific areas of our lives. He will reveal the passionate affections in God's heart for us in ways that are incredibly wonderful, vividly real and perfectly tailored to fit our own understanding and personal experience.

Good examples and zeal didn't produce passionate love for Christ in me. I was an angry, frustrated Christian who constantly carried a heavy burden of guilt and failure for not measuring up and not enjoying serving others. Only when I caught a glimpse of the true knowledge of how God really felt about me did the strongholds fall in my mind and in my heart. These words came to mind, "Herein is our love made perfect, that we may have boldness in the day of judgment: because as he is, so are we in this world. There is no fear in love; but perfect love casteth out fear: because fear hath torment" (1 John 4:17-18, KJV).

I saw that the person who was afraid of God, who feared His judgment of their failings, lived in torment. Torment is the opposite of boldness with a tenderized heart for God. And I had to recognize that God's heart was filled with tenderness for me — even though I wasn't perfect.

God, who has never painted the same sunset twice, knows exactly how to reveal Himself to you. He will choose the perfect time and place to speak to you. He knows the precise revelations of Himself that will illuminate your understanding, feed your hungry heart or flow like warm, healing oil over your wounded spirit.

When you come to your heavenly Father for help, you will not be ignored or rebuked. You will not be ridiculed for your mistakes. He is extraordinarily patient toward you. He cares for you affectionately and watchfully. His love for you will never fail or come to an end.

It's wonderful to have known people who showed us what God is really like. Their examples can help prepare the way for God's work in our lives or even speed up the process. But if we have never known even one loving, godly person, we can still experience personal wholeness and be filled with passionate affections for Jesus. God, His Word and the Holy Spirit's work in our lives are sufficient to bring us to personal wholeness and spiritual maturity.

Recovering the True Knowledge of God

What will cure the "hundred lesser evils that are everywhere among us"[3]? It is the knowledge of God's personality. Knowing how He views us in Christ will strengthen the inner man and demolish Satan's strongholds. Christianity must become God-centered. We must recover that lofty concept of God and rediscover His majesty. We must practice the art of long and loving meditation on the truths of the Scriptures and the being of God. Only one thing will ever satisfy our deep cravings. We must come to know God as He is: the excellencies of His person; His extravagant passions; and His ravished heart.

The church knows Jesus as her Savior. But the Son of God is getting ready to reveal Himself as her beloved, clothed in majesty and splendor. His love will ignite the passions of His people. A terminally bored church is about to be swept off her feet!

SEVEN

Igniting
Holy Passion

The Ravished Heart of God: Part 1

A faithful Christian woman in her early forties gathered the courage after many years to resign from her job, leave the home of her godly parents and go to work for a missions organization overseas. Molested as a child, she had lived much of her life controlled by fear. She had not yet overcome her fears, but her sparkling eyes and bubbly personality covered up her lack of confidence and low self-esteem.

She longed to marry a godly Christian and serve the Lord

with him, but the right man had never come along. The woman was therefore surprised and pleased when a single Christian man about her age who worked for the same missions group began showing her attention — warm smiles; genuine appreciation for her conscientious work; little compliments dropped here and there. She was even more surprised when he suggested that they begin having lunch together several times a week.

She felt so plain. So ordinary. So undesirable. But the more the woman got to know her new friend, the more she liked and respected him. She could tell the feelings were mutual.

One day at work the man asked if he could take her out for dinner. That evening she glanced up from the menu and saw him gazing at her with a tender, loving expression in his eyes. "I'm sorry for staring," he said, a little embarrassed, "but you are so beautiful that you take my breath away."

The woman could hardly believe her ears. Beautiful! Me? She opened her mouth to protest and put herself down, but something stopped her. *He sees you the way I see you*, an inner thought seemed to say. Overwhelmed beyond words, the woman's face broke into a radiant smile.

How do you think God sees you? Do you cringe at the thought? God's estimation of your beauty comes from His great love for you — not as a result of any inherent goodness or beauty of your own.

God is not the cold, aloof, rigidly legalistic being that religion has made Him out to be. He is not the demanding, impatient God so many of us have struggled to please. Oh, how the Lord longs for His church to receive a revelation of His ravished heart — utterly overwhelmed with delight for us — even though we may not like or believe in ourselves. How His heart aches for us to become aware of His fascination with our beauty and respond to His yearning glance (Ps. 45:11).

Our God is not a thing or an it. He is an affectionate, loving, deeply passionate being. Today's church desperately needs a renewed understanding of the nature of God's personality and a deeper comprehension of His extravagant passion.

The Missing Dimension of Our Redemption

The Reformers and their successors radically transformed Christianity by rediscovering the essential truth of the gospel — we are justified by faith alone.

What a liberating experience it was for people to understand that the gift of righteousness could be received simply by faith. It was like coming out of darkness into the daylight. Salvation involves a glorious exchange in which Christ takes our sin and guilt, and we take on His righteousness. I love the doctrines of salvation, sanctification and adoption that highlight our legal position in Christ. I believe they are a vital dimension to the preaching of the cross and are foundational to a healthy walk with God.

But reformed evangelicalism can also become rigid and scholastic. The whole of one's relationship with God is often defined in terms of legal standing with Him and His law. God is the judge who stamps *accepted* on our foreheads, then turns and says, "Next!" That's good news, but that is not all the good news. In a relationship defined by law, a believer is never made aware of a God whose heart is overwhelmed and ravished — enraptured and filled with delight — by His people.

Salvation is more than a legal exchange affecting our position before God. Salvation also includes the exchange of deep loving affections and adoration. God first communicates His enjoyment, longing and affections for us and, in turn, we respond in a similar way. As John said, "We love Him because He first loved us" (1 John 4:19, NKJV).

An intellectual understanding of the legal aspects alone is not enough. Why? Because we will never have more affection or passion for God than we understand He has for us. We will never be more committed to God than our understanding of His commitment to us.

The Holy Spirit must quicken the knowledge of God's passionate love and make it alive in our hearts — a God whose personality overflows with extravagant emotions for His people. The loving, passionate heart of God must pulsate at the core of all our ministry, whether it be teaching others how to be saved, ministering to the sick or leading a home group.

Although God is totally self-sufficient, He desires our love. He, who has no need of us, has bound His heart to us forever.

> In this is love, not that we loved God, but that He loved us and sent His Son to be the propitiation for our sins (1 John 4:10, NKJV).

The affectionate, passionate heart of God swells with joy and delight over us even while we're failing and being self-centered. Everybody knows God loves us when we're mature, when we're conformed to His image. But God loves and enjoys us even when we are *not* like Him, when we are coming up short in actual victory even though our hearts are sincerely reaching out for Him.

The book of Romans contains the *legal, earthly, practical dimension* of our redemption. The book of Revelation reveals the *eternal, majestic dimension* of our redemption. The Song of Solomon extols the *passionate, affectionate dimension* of our redemption. All three of these dimensions will come together in a thorough understanding of our relationship to God as mentioned in Psalm 2:11-12 (NKJV).

> Serve the Lord with fear, and rejoice with trembling.
> Kiss the Son, lest He be angry, and you perish in
>   the way.

We rejoice for the free gift of salvation in Romans, tremble at His majesty in Revelation and kiss the Son in response to His affection as revealed in the Song of Solomon.

The Song of Solomon, the King's song to His bride, needs to be taught and sung with revelation and power. It will wash and restore the church, as it prophetically calls her forth to holy passion.

The Song of Solomon can be interpreted on several different levels. Historically, it depicts the wooing and wedding of a shepherdess by King Solomon. In terms of typology, it pictures Israel as God's espoused bride in the same way that the church is pictured as the bride of Christ in the New Testament. Some say it describes the love of a natural man for his wife. Others see it as a true story written in symbolic language with spiritual meaning for believers today.

Personally, I believe the Holy Spirit can interpret the book to the church in all these different ways, and we can learn from each of them. But I want to share with you the way the book has edified me.

The Progression of Holy Passion

In this love song from heaven, I picture the maiden as the young maturing church, the bride of Christ. I see a clear spiritual progression in the eight chapters of the Song of Solomon. It is a divine pattern revealing the progression of holy passion in the heart of the church as she is wooed and subdued by the beauty and splendor of her glorious King.

There are at least two wonderful benefits from meditating upon this great prophetic song of redemptive history.

First, the Holy Spirit unveils to us the passions and pleasures in the personality of the Son of God. This new insight into the heart of Jesus captures our hearts in a fresh way, and our spirits are energized and opened to new depths of passion for Him.

Second, as we meditate upon the Song of Solomon we identify our present position in this divine pattern of progression toward Christian maturity. As we begin to understand the purpose in God's difficult dealings with us, we are comforted and refreshed, and our spirits are washed. This new comprehension brings increased ability to cooperate courageously and confidently with the Spirit's work in us.

The Awakening to Fervency —
Song of Solomon 1:2

There must come a time in the lives of mature believers when we are awakened to holy fervency. When we cry, "God, I'm tired of serving You from a distance. I don't care what it's going to cost me. I want to be wholly Yours in the deepest part of my being."

I will never forget the feeling that flooded my being when I realized that the great invisible God who created the earth and all that is in it — including me — actually listened to me when I talked to Him. He actually responded to my requests. He answered scores of little prayers for me.

Once when I was leading a college ministry ski trip, five people who did not have the money wanted to come on the trip. I told them they could come, even when I didn't have the money to pay for them either. I cried out to the Lord for help. Someone who knew about the ski trip but knew nothing of the need approached me on the day we were to leave and offered me a check for two thousand dollars, if I needed it.

This was a stunning example in the early days of God's care for me. That realization sparked a flame of fervency within my spirit that has never been extinguished — and never will.

The progression of passion starts with this fresh awakening to holy fervency. But fervency by itself is not maturity. It is only the beginning.

The Song of Solomon opens with the great prophetic cry of the Spirit in the church today: "May he kiss me with the kisses of his mouth! For your love is better than wine" (Song 1:2). This speaks figuratively of the awakened believer's cry for the "kiss of intimacy," not just the casual kiss on the cheek from a relative or friend. Spiritually it speaks of the cry for deeper intimacy with God.

Believers today are realizing that if our hunger for intimacy is ever to be satisfied, we must have Him whose affectionate love is far better than "churchianity" or the best wine of earthly experiences and possessions. Like the maiden who cried, "Your love is better than wine," believers are coming to the point where they realize that money and material things are never going to supply the needs of our spirits. Prominence in the church or the world will never do it. No sensual or romantic relationship with another human being will ever satisfy the deep cravings of our spirits. We're becoming tired of powerless religion that can't deliver us from sin or from ourselves; tired of leaders filled with anger, striving and immorality; tired of churches paralyzed in apathy. We're weary of trying to draw water from a dry well in the name of Jesus.

An abandonment, a holy recklessness, is awakening in the spirits of God's people. The Spirit of God is calling us forth, taking the truths of time and eternity and using them to awaken us out of complacency. Before this world comes to an end, God will raise up a church full of people who are hungering for God-centered religion from among those who are satisfied with man-centered Christianity. The denominational label won't matter. If the Son of God is being ministered in power, and His personal beauty and loveliness are unveiled, people will flock to Him.

Why do we want Him? We've discovered that the love and affection of God are better than anything the world has to offer, and we're beginning to see a little bit of the splendor, majesty and matchless beauty of Christ Jesus.

> Because of the fragrance of your good ointments, your name is ointment poured forth (Song 1:3, NKJV).

The lovely perfumed fragrance speaks symbolically of the graces of Christ's personality, the beauty of who He is and the perfection of all He does. The irresistible aroma of His perfume will capture the church again.

> We love Him because He first loved us (1 John 4:19, NKJV).

It takes God to love God. It takes a progressive revelation of God's infinitely satisfying love, His exuberant affections and His indescribable beauty to awaken the church and compel her to give herself wholly back to Him. Like Paul, believers will be compelled by this knowledge of God's love (2 Cor. 5:14).

Some believers look at others who have high-energy personalities and say, "If I were wired with 220 volts like you, I'd be filled with zeal and passion for God, too. But I have a totally different temperament. I'm one of those 110-volt folks." Passion for Jesus is not a personality trait. You can have the gentlest human makeup possible and still be consumed with the fire of God. You may not express your passion in the same way a "220-volt" type personality does, but that fiery devotion will be there, and it will be just as real.

It doesn't matter how much human energy or natural zeal we possess. Passion for Jesus is the fruit of recognizing His dedication to us — not the fruit of our dedication to Him. We will walk in a life of commitment to Him because He is committed to us. When we stand before God, not a person on earth will be able to say, "I gave more to You than You gave to me."

Most of us have known some superspiritual people who got hyped up for a year or two. But over the long haul, when the trials and tribulations hit, all that frothy human zeal fizzled out.

I recall my own experience with a team of street preachers involved in campus ministry. Some of these radical, zealous evangelists preached fiery sermons on the college campuses during the sixties and seventies. But ten years later they weren't even walking with God. Their extraordinary zeal had led nowhere — except away from God.

Their commitment to Jesus was limited by an incomplete revelation of His commitment to His people. He is absolutely abandoned and totally committed to those who are His.

Our fervency for the Lord delights His heart. He knows the presence of fervency is not the same as spiritual maturity. Many fervent believers still do not understand even the central issues of the gospel. That's OK. Christ Jesus loves His people. He loves their fervency, even though we may still make messes because of our immaturity. In His heart He is absolutely in love with us.

Prioritizing Intimacy and Ministry — Song of Solomon 1:4

After the maiden in the Song of Solomon awakens to fervency, she prays a twofold prayer: "Draw me after you and let us run together" (Song 1:4). The order of that prayer is very important. First we are drawn to Him in intimacy, then we run with Him in ministry. If we are to become colaborers with Christ, running with Him, we should first focus on being drawn as worshippers, consecrated in purity with affectionate passions.

It's easy to pray, "Let me run. Increase my sphere of ministry and influence," without also fervently seeking the Lord to draw us near to Him. But as we are drawn to greater intimacy with God, we have a greater spiritual depth and touch other people's spirits more effectively. That is what "running," or real ministry, is all about — bringing deliverance to the hearts of human beings so they can know and worship God intimately, too.

On the other hand, some believers say, "Draw me," but never go on to run with the Lord as a partner with Him in His work in the earth. The Holy Spirit does not draw us so we can hang up a "Do Not Disturb" sign and sit in our little comfort zone singing love songs to Jesus the rest of our lives. As fellow heirs with Christ, we are drawn into intimacy, then empowered in ministry to bring others into intimacy with the Lord.

I believe the church will mature in this difficult tension of drawing and running. We will learn how to deliver broken people, prevail in spiritual warfare and serve one another while maintaining our intimacy with Jesus. These two prayers, to be drawn and to run, correspond to the two great commandments Jesus gave in Matthew 22:37-40.

Being drawn into deep intimacy with Jesus fulfills the first commandment to love God with all our hearts, and running in servanthood ministry fulfills the second commandment to love our neighbors as ourselves

Your Life Goal

In the first chapter of this beautiful song of love we saw where the maiden stated her intention (vv. 1-4). She laid out the goal and theme of her life on earth. She desired an intimate relationship with him whose love was better to her than the best wine of the world. Then from verse 5 all the way to the end of the book, we trace the maiden's unbroken journey in her progression of passion for her beloved.

For over twenty years I've remained committed to the life vision that I received in my first year of college. Even though I enrolled in college with the goal of becoming a medical doctor, that was merely my vocational vision. My greater life vision held this twofold purpose: becoming a worshipper of God and a deliverer of men. In other words, to love God and to love my neighbor.

On my first date with Diane, I remember blurting out the highest desire of my heart: "Diane, somewhere in life — whether I'm a doctor, a schoolteacher, a preacher or whatever — I want to be a worshipper of God and a deliverer of men."

My vocational vision changed. I left Washington University just thirty days after I began when my brother, Pat, broke his neck. Although I was later given verbal acceptance into a six-year medical program, I asked God to confirm this move through my father. On the last day before I had to verify my acceptance into this program, my father said, "I feel as if it's really wrong for you to do this six-year medical program."

Dad was never aware that he was the answer to my prayer for confirmation, but my vocational vision changed. God subsequently led me to become a pastor — not a doctor. But my life vision has never changed.

It's important that you and I have goals. But we need to have one life goal that all our other goals serve. If you don't know what your life goal is, ask the Lord to show you. Ask Him to draw you into intimacy with Him, then to empower your ministry of servanthood so that whatever you do, wherever you go, you can help bring others into intimacy with Jesus.

Is your spirit longing for a new awakening to the wonderful, satisfying love of God? Do you want to know Him intimately?

> *O Lord, we have seen just a little bit of Your splendor and majesty. The beauty of who You are and what You do is capturing our hearts like a lovely, irresistible fragrance. From this point on I want my life to be one unbroken journey of progression in holy passion. Draw me, Lord. Draw me to Your glorious self. I don't want to be at a distance. I want You, no matter what it costs me. Draw me, Jesus, and I will run after You!*

And as I run, I will learn to mature in obedience. But how?

EIGHT

Fervent — But Immature

The Ravished Heart of God: Part 2

When I begin to comprehend God's overwhelming love for me, passion for Jesus awakens inside me. Initially this progression toward spiritual maturity is sincere and fervently devout. Nevertheless, my commitment to the Lord may be much more superficial than I realize at first.

Like the maiden in the Song of Solomon, I have experienced difficulty in prioritizing intimacy and ministry. In my early life as a Christian I was more interested in studying the

Word and witnessing to unbelievers than I was in spending quality time alone with God in devotional prayer. My heart grew cold because of this.

Even today, in the busyness of a growing church, my heart is pulled away from retreating in private to my secret life with God. My wife, Diane, holds me accountable for this time, as I do for her. We constantly challenge each other to balance our ministry with our intimate times with God.

Like the maiden, all believers pass through a self-centered stage where our goals are focused on receiving blessings and experiencing Christ's presence. Blessings and the thrill of spiritual experiences are perfectly legitimate, but they are not the final goal of mature Christianity.

Living in the Pleasure of His Presence — Song of Solomon 2:3-6

In the following verses, notice the maiden's emphasis on the pleasure she is experiencing personally. I can imagine her exclaiming, "Just me and Jesus! This is awesome."

> In his shade *I took great delight* and sat down,
> And his fruit was *sweet to my taste.*
> He has *brought me to his banquet hall,*
> And his banner over me is love.
> *Sustain me* with raisin cakes,
> *Refresh me* with apples,
> Because *I* am lovesick.
> Let his left hand be under *my* head
> And his right hand *embrace me* (Song 2:3-6, italics
>   added).

Discovering that Jesus is the essential source of spiritual delight is an important part of our progression toward maturity, and the Lord does not want that process disturbed. He leaves us right where we are for a season; growing in the knowledge of His loveliness and faithfulness and feeling increasingly secure and satisfied.

At this stage, we don't really know what's going on. We're thinking only of receiving our inheritance from God, not of being His eternal inheritance. As far as we're concerned, Jesus is reigning in heaven solely for our pleasure. We know little about His passion to disciple the nations, little about faith that embraces risk and sacrifice and little about warfare.

But while we are discovering His beauty and delighting ourselves in Him, the Lord is sealing our spirits. We will never again be content with a life of compromise that neglects spiritual intimacy. The knowledge of His commitment and abandonment to us awakens our commitment back to Him and begins to develop the maturity in which we will walk in days to come.

Jesus may allow us to spend months or even years in this spiritually satisfying, secure, self-absorbed stage. Sometimes, knowing just a little of God's passionate personality, we can make the mistake of assuming we've arrived. But being saved and spiritually satisfied is only part of our inheritance. The other part is that we are equipped and matured to be co-heirs and share Christ's heart, His home, His throne forever.

We have an inheritance in God, but God also has an inheritance in us. What an incredible thought: God, who possesses everything, has something He waits for — His inheritance in us (Eph. 1:11,18).

Challenging the Comfort Zone —
Song of Solomon 2:8-17

Little by little in this progression of holy passion, we begin to figure out that fervency is not the same as full maturity. Because the Lord loves us so affectionately and so deeply, He gives us a whole new revelation of Himself.

At this stage of this beautiful song of love, the maiden

suddenly sees her beloved in an entirely different dimension. She watches as he comes to her, leaping and skipping like a gazelle.

> The voice of my beloved!
> Behold, he comes
> Leaping upon the mountains,
> Skipping upon the hills (Song 2:8, NKJV).

The hills and mountains speak of obstacles that must be overcome. They include trials and tribulations of Christian growth. They also refer to our struggle against satanic principalities and powers. These obstacles may be the kingdoms of this world that oppose the gospel. It doesn't matter. No obstacle is insurmountable for our God.

Her beloved comes and stands outside, speaking to the maiden through a window in the wall. He asks her to arise and come away with him, for the flowers have appeared, the time has come for pruning the vines, and the fig tree has ripened its figs (Song 2:10-13). This refers to the time of preparation just before the harvest.

But she replies: "Turn, my beloved, and be like a gazelle or a young stag upon the mountains" (Song 2:17).

Like the maiden, you and I, in the early stages of spiritual passion, may have seen Jesus as the only One whose beauty satisfies our hearts. Maybe we've not yet seen our Beloved as the Sovereign King who effortlessly leaps over mountains and hills as He exercises His authority over the nations, displaying His mighty power over everything that opposes Him.

We first know Him as our satisfying Savior and provider who gives us great delight at His loving banquet table under His shade tree. The One who answers our prayers and meets our needs. But eventually we encounter Him as the mighty Lord who skips on mountains and hills. Do you remember when you and the Lord had an encounter similar to this one where He challenged you to arise and leave your spiritual comfort zone?

You asked, "Why were You skipping over those hills and mountains? I like the comfortable corner with just You and me."

"I want you to come with Me in warfare and in sacrificial service," He replied. " 'Arise, My darling, My beautiful one and come along' [Song 2:10]. You can't sit under the shade tree forever. Come and leap mountains and skip hills with Me. I know you love Me. But will you love Me enough to help release others from bondage and bring them into a deep, affectionate relationship with Me, even though such a life is inconvenient, risky and self-sacrificing?"

I must admit that I've answered Him much like this: "But, Lord, I can't go. I don't want to leave our apple tree and our banquet table. It took me years to get to the place where I really enjoyed just being with You, Lord, and I don't want to lose it. I love You; I'm happy and satisfied. I have new kingdom relationships that are so rewarding and satisfying. Let someone else reach out to others and disciple the nations. I only want to be with You."

Just like the maiden in the Song of Solomon, I have sometimes refused Christ's challenge and told Him to go away and skip and leap on the mountains by Himself (Song 2:17).

It was 1982 in St. Louis. I had completed seven years of church planting. I was comfortably content in a church of five hundred adults. I was only twenty-seven, and the congregation was young, athletic and enthusiastic about my leadership.

Then the Lord showed me that I was to turn that church over to the leadership team and move to Kansas City. I was miserable. I didn't want to lose all my friends. I had been so content at that church. Even an old pastor-friend advised me to stay there. I wrestled with God every moment of every day. I couldn't pray or worship.

There was such a clear sense of the withdrawing of His

peace that, after two weeks, I could stand it no longer. In the middle of the night I finally promised the Lord I would go.

When I accepted this challenge from Christ I was immediately filled with the sweetness of His love. I spent several days in heightened fellowship with my Lord.

Out of your fear and human weakness, have you ever told the Lord no when He asked you to do something for Him? I believe that's why the maiden we've been studying refused to go with her beloved. It wasn't stubbornness or rebellion. It was just human weakness. She was fervent — but immature. Like the maiden, you and I can be in relationship with our Beloved for our own spiritual pleasure, not to become a mature, spiritual disciple existing for His pleasure and purpose.

Experiencing the Lord's Correction — Song of Solomon 3:1-3

The Lord isn't angered and exasperated by our human weakness. That's all we have to give Him. That's all He has to work with. But if we refuse to obey the Lord, He must lovingly discipline us. When we ask the Lord, as the maiden did in chapter 1, verse 4, to draw us and let us run together with Him, that means leaving our secure little comfort zone and going to the mountains with Him when He asks.

Sometimes the Lord corrects us and gets our attention by gently withdrawing His presence for a season. That is the way the maiden's beloved dealt with her reluctance to follow him.

> On my bed night after night I sought him
> Whom my soul loves;
> I sought him but did not find him.
> I must arise now and go about the city;
> In the streets and in the squares
> I must seek him whom my soul loves.
> I sought him but did not find him.

> The watchmen who make the rounds in the city
>   found me,
> And I said, "Have you seen him whom my soul
>   loves?" (Song 3:1-3).

When the Lord corrects us in that manner, He is not angry with us. He still loves and enjoys us in our immaturity. However, He loves us too much to let us hold on to a life of spiritual immaturity. Although we do not understand it, He is bringing us forth to maturity. He knows what awaits us — the glory of being His bride and the wondrous spiritual treasures in store for us as mature co-heirs of the glorious Son of God.

Therefore, He gently pries our fingers loose from the things we're clinging to so tenaciously. Firmly, but tenderly, He woos us away from anything that would hold us back from His best. He says to us, "If you knew the glory of all I am and all you are to be, you would never refuse Me. Have I ever led you into a place where I could not keep you and provide for you? I will never take anything from you that will not be restored tenfold. My disciplines are good. They seem sorrowful for the moment, but afterward they yield the fruit of righteousness" (see Heb. 12:5-13).

After this time of gentle discipline, the maiden arises from her bed under the shade tree and searches until she finds her beloved (Song 3:2-4). When the Lord's presence departs from us in our place of compromise, just like this maiden, you and I must arise in obedience and faith and seek Him. I think I know what she said when she found her beloved. I've had to say it to the Lord a few times myself, such as when He wanted me to move to Kansas City and His peace had left so distinctly: "OK, You win. I must have Your presence. What is comfort, what is security, without Your presence?"

Affirming and Wooing the Bride —
Song of Solomon 4:1-5

Now wedded and united with her in love, the maiden's bridegroom exclaims, "How beautiful you are, my darling. How beautiful you are." Then he speaks specific prophetic affirmations, wooing his bride to come forth (Song 4:1-5). In the same way, Jesus, our glorious Bridegroom, speaks prophetically over us as we timidly arise and take baby steps forward, purposing to leave the comfort zone and progress into more maturity. He does not condemn us for our immaturity or accuse us of our failures. Instead, He calls things that are not as though they were, because He sees those things in seed form in our hearts (Rom. 4:17).

We see our failures and shortcomings, and we think God is against us, accusing and condemning us. The devil has deceived us, leading us to attribute to God what is true of himself. Satan, not God, is the accuser of the brethren. God is our affirmer — our encourager. He believes in our sincere desires to obey Him more than we do and calls us forth in ways we would never dream. He says, "I love you! I have passionate affections for you! I will transform a fervent, immature maiden into My reigning, mature bride."

The turning point in the maiden's life comes right here in chapter 4, verse 6. The beautiful words just spoken over her by her beloved have awakened a growing confidence and an unwavering resolve in the maiden's heart and have called her into increasing fullness. She declares, "I will go my way to the mountain of myrrh and to the hill of frankincense." Similarly, Christ's affirming, prophetic words spoken over our spirits awaken confidence and resolve in us and call us to obey Him fully.

Embracing the Cross —
Song of Solomon 4:6-7

In chapter 2, the maiden said no to the hills and mountains, but now she is ready to go to the mountain of myrrh and the hill of frankincense (Song 4:6). Myrrh, used in preparing a body for burial, and frankincense, which does not give forth its fragrant perfume until it is burned, were two of the gifts laden with prophetic meaning that were given by the wise men to Jesus at His birth. The gifts spoke prophetically of His suffering and death on the cross. Here, the maiden is speaking figuratively of the suffering and death of her beloved. She is saying what you and I must say if we are to experience greater maturity in the Lord: "I want only to be like You. I will embrace the cross. I will not refuse You again. I will arise and go my way to the mountain of myrrh and the hills of frankincense."

Some people think the will of God is always hard, but that's not true. The will of God is good, satisfying and perfect (Rom. 12:2). We find tremendous pleasure, fulfillment and joy in the will of God. On the other hand, there are times when we must say no to the desires of our flesh, times when our own carnal passions conflict with the will of God. At such times, we must deny ourselves.

That is what Jesus meant when He said, "If anyone wishes to come after Me, let him deny himself, and take up his cross daily, and follow Me" (Luke 9:23). He said we cannot be His disciples if we don't do this. If we want to be colaborers with Jesus, fulfilling His purposes in the earth, we must step out of the comfort zone and move into the life of faith where our only source is the invisible God and the integrity of His Word.

Did you notice the maiden said, "I will go *my way* to the mountain of myrrh..." (Song 4:6, italics added)? The cross you embrace will be different from the cross another person is called to embrace. Trying to embrace another's cross may result in legalism. What is an easy yoke of obedience for one believer may become a religious burden for another who embraces what God has not called that believer to.

The grace of God has gifted my life with the ability to intercede for many other individuals. But I tried to force that yoke on the members of my church. I preached to others that they *must* spend much time in intercession for others. They tried to respond but became burdened and burned-out because they were merely being forced to bear my yoke.

You and I must each "go our own ways" to the mountain of myrrh. When God asks us to carry a cross, He also supplies us with grace and a sense of personal conviction that is needed to carry it. The yoke is easy, joyful and light when He puts it on us.

As we begin to know the excellencies of the personality of the Lord, we, like this maiden, feel increasingly secure. "You are a safe God," we say. "I'm not afraid anymore. I may lose my job and my house. I may lose my reputation. I know You're not promising I can keep everything I have now. Nevertheless, I will joyfully go with You to the mountain of myrrh and the hill of frankincense because I trust You, Lord."

The response of her beloved to the maiden's commitment to him is so wonderful: "You are altogether beautiful, my darling, and there is no blemish in you" (Song 4:7). The truth of the matter is that the progression of spiritual maturity in the Song of Solomon still has four chapters to go — the maiden has not fully matured. But her beloved, like ours, looks at the intention of the heart and exclaims, "There is no blemish in you. You are altogether beautiful!"

I can imagine a conversation with our Lord.

"Oh, Lord, I slandered someone today."

"Yes, but when you slandered, you called it sin and cried out for forgiveness, didn't you?"

"Well, yes. But...."

"There's no spot in you, My darling. Your heart is reaching out to Mine in sincerity and integrity, and you trust Me."

"Oh, yes. I really want to know You, Lord. I have sought deeper intimacy with You, but I thought You'd be angry with me for slandering."

"I was grieved when you did it, but you repented. You cast it down and called it your enemy."

"Yes, I did. Does that mean You still like me?"

"*Like* you? My heart is overflowing with affectionate love and extravagant passion for you!"

"But I'm still such a mess, I make so many mistakes and I'm always blowing it."

"I know that, but it is My devoted, passionate heart that will bring you to maturity."

Can you sense the renewed commitment to maturity that this conversation between the Lord and His beloved would invoke?

Even when we are weak, even when we fail, the Lord looks at the sincerity and devotion of our hearts and exclaims, "You are so beautiful to Me!" The knowledge that Jesus continues to enjoy us as we are maturing is a foundational truth that empowers us to mature.

Equipping the Soul for the Tests Ahead —
Song of Solomon 4:7-10

For the first time, the maiden is now called the "bride." She is now beginning to mature to the place where she may function as the bride and co-heir. The maturity in greater levels of spiritual warfare is now manifest. Her beloved says:

Come with me from Lebanon, my bride...
Journey down from the summit...
From the dens of lions,
From the mountains of leopards (Song 4:8).

Lions and leopards are devouring animals. This verse is speaking figuratively of engaging in higher levels of spiritual warfare requiring greater steps of sacrifice and servanthood. Satan, that roaring lion, often lets sleeping saints lie. But when we're seeking to walk in obedience and to invade the enemy's territory aggressively, he launches a fierce counter-attack against us.

When I hear people talk about spiritual warfare casually, I

think: You obviously haven't been assaulted very powerfully by the devil before! I don't mind getting in the battle, but I'm going to advance wisely and cautiously. I know we can use the Word of God against Satan, but it's a real fight of faith — not a game. Sometimes his counterattack against us can last hours, weeks or even months. We think, Wait a minute, Lord. I was never confronted with this level of assault when I was comfortable on lower ground.

I have observed this as teams of young people have traveled to Muslim countries on missions trips. Young and excited, they are challenged to minister on the streets to people steeped in satanic culture. Many times they have not understood the enemy's tactics and were thus unprepared for the warfare. They come home disillusioned and disappointed because they failed to count the cost.

Taking ground from the enemy and holding on to it require tenacity and resolution of the heart. Satan pushes, resists and fights back every step of the way.

Our church has planted six congregations in the Kansas City area. Each time I prepared for a breakout of trouble, extra conflict and the resulting weariness. And we had it!

So when the Lord mentions skipping on mountains and encountering lions and leopards, I don't cheer and say, "Great! This is gonna be fun!" A soberness comes into my spirit. I know I'm going to have to keep alert with my mind renewed and my thoughts obedient, or my flesh is going to become very weary.

Aware of the sorrows and spiritual battles just ahead, the maiden's beloved sounds the same warning that Jesus sometimes gives us: "Lions and leopards — dark powers and principalities — will be roaring in the night. You'll be going all the way to embrace the cross at the mountain of myrrh and the hill of frankincense. This will be costly." But like you and me, the bride has set her soul to embrace fully the will of her beloved. She looks at him, and her eyes reflect the deep love and unwavering resolve in her heart for him whom her soul loves. She has made the decision to entrust and abandon herself to him, no matter what the cost.

The Ravished Heart of God

Her beloved cries,

> You have ravished my heart,
> My sister, my spouse;
> You have ravished my heart
> With one look of your eyes (Song 4:9, NKJV).

What does it mean to "ravish" the heart?

According to the dictionary, the word *ravish* means "to seize and take away by violence; to overcome with emotions of joy or delight; unusually attractive, pleasing or striking."

The bride had captured his heart, filling it with ecstasy and delight. One look from her eyes had seized his heart and carried it away. "Your love has overwhelmed me," he is exclaiming. "You are so strikingly beautiful, so utterly pleasing to me!"

The bride wasn't mature yet, but as she heard her beloved wooing and affirming her, her fears melted away, and she was given courage to follow him. Remember: All she has done at this point is say yes. She hasn't fully waged war with the enemy. Yet she has ravished and conquered the heart of her beloved with her sincere yes to him and her loving glance.

This is exactly what happens to the heart of Jesus when you and I look unto Him and set our souls to follow Him at any cost. "You have ravished My heart with one look from your eyes," He exclaims. "I am overwhelmed by your devotion. You are so beautiful, so utterly delightful. You have captured My heart."

Did you know that your yes to Christ — your immature, but sincere, commitment to Him — utterly ravishes His heart?

Even though your actions sometimes fall short of your intentions, the devout resolution of your heart overwhelms Him with affectionate emotion. He looks at you and yearns over you, longing to draw you into a more intimate relationship with Him.

It is this revelation of Jesus' ravished heart for you that awakens your heart to fervency for Him, igniting your progression in holy passion. And it is His passionate love for you and your response of love and devotion for Him that act as a breastplate of love, guarding your heart with holy affections in times of temptation and in the difficult hours of life (1 Thess. 5:8).

Learning to Discern the Right Voice

God calls us forth in ways we would never dream, yet we accuse ourselves so terribly. Perhaps you have grown so accustomed to the constant, condemning barrage from the enemy, from your own accusing thoughts or the criticism of others, you hardly know what it is like to live without a sense of sin, failure and rejection clouding your heart. You may have come to view yourself as failing, utterly unlovely and worthless, but that is not the way your beloved Lord sees you.

I have a pastor friend who after fifteen years of ministry made some mistakes in issues of character and discretion. For five years after his mistakes, he could only imagine a God who was angry with him, who was constantly holding him in judgment. Though he led many others to the Lord during this time and brought deliverance to his people, he could only find judgment in his own life. Through personal counseling times and hearing the Word and believing it, he began to see himself as God saw him — passionately loved and forgiven. Only then could he feel once more the enjoyment that the Lord had in him.

As you look to Jesus and set your soul to follow Him at

any cost, one loving glance seizes His heart and carries it away. "You have ravished My heart with one look from your eyes!" He exclaims. "I am overwhelmed by your devotion. You are so lovely, such a source of joy and delight to My heart!"

Every time Satan comes to weight down your heart and depress your spirit with his lies, turn a deaf ear. The next time your own heart points a merciless, judgmental finger because you are not perfect and fully mature, simply turn away and listen to the loving voice of Jesus instead.

"You are so pleasing, so beautiful to Me, so utterly delightful," you will hear Him say. "You have captured My heart!"

And when you hear the affectionate, affirming words of your Beloved, don't open your mouth to protest. Accept them. Believe them. They're really true. His desire is to unveil His heart to you as we will see next.

NINE

The Secret Garden

The Ravished Heart of God: Part 3

The beloved has revealed his ravished heart to his bride, but he has much more to say to her. Aware that the bride is not yet ready for the critical tests just ahead, the beloved continues to affirm the bride, expressing his great affection for her. This is a very important spiritual principle that has application for you and me as believers. The knowledge of God's love and affection prepares us to experience His fullness and to remain strong and faithful to Him in times of persecution and testing.

Equipping and Calling Forth Into Increasing Fullness — Song of Solomon 4:10-12

In the Song of Solomon the beloved lavishes his love upon his bride. He describes the qualities of his maturing bride, telling how exceedingly precious her inner thoughts, words and deeds are to him:

> How much better than wine is your love,
> And the scent of your perfumes
> Than all spices!
> Your lips, O my spouse,
> Drip as the honeycomb;
> Honey and milk are under your tongue;
> And the fragrance of your garments
> Is like the fragrance of Lebanon.
> A garden enclosed
> Is my sister, my spouse,
> A spring shut up,
> A fountain sealed (Song 4:10-12, NKJV).

Earlier, the bride told her beloved that his love for her was better than wine (Song 1:2, NKJV). Now he gazes longingly and tenderly at her and reverses her statement by saying, "How much better than wine is your love."

Jesus declares that our love for Him is better than wine — better than all the kingdoms of the world, better than all the glorious works of His hands. Truly, the heart of Jesus is utterly ravished by the resolute heart, the loving abandonment of His church for Him.

The beloved finds wonderful delight in his beautiful bride in three ways — her perfume, the sweetness of her lips, the fragrance of her garments. There is a symbolic meaning here for you and me.

A Fragrance of Thoughts and Prayers Before the Throne

The scent of the bride's perfume can represent her inner

thought life which emanates as a lovely fragrance to the Lord. God hears the secret cry of our spirits that no one else hears, and it ascends as a beautiful perfume before Him. God alone sees the secret thoughts and intentions of our hearts as we long to please Him, even when we are failing spiritually.

In John's vision recorded in the book of Revelation there were golden bowls full of incense carried by the twenty-four elders and the four creatures. These bowls were "full of incense, which are the prayers of the saints" (Rev. 5:8). The cry of the saints to their Beloved is as a fragrant incense to the Lord.

I love the words of David: "You number my wanderings; put my tears into Your bottle; are they not in Your book?" (Ps. 56:8, NKJV). David was weeping over his own failings, just as I wept when I realized what my anger and bitterness over serving others did to the Lord. But those tears of repentance and sorrow were precious to Him.

Instead of condemning ourselves and other Christians who weaken or fall, you and I need to realize that the tears of broken believers are very dear and precious to God. When we get to heaven, I wouldn't be surprised if a conversation much like this takes place:

"Oh, Lord, You know I sinned and failed You thousands of times as I served You on earth."

"Yes, that's true," the Lord will respond. "But what you didn't realize was that I heard the moans and sobs of your spirit when you failed Me. I saw every tear as it trickled down your cheek."

"Honest, Lord? You really mean it? How could I have been so confused? Half the time I wasn't even sure if You loved me or not. Sometimes I wasn't even sure if I loved You."

"I knew that," He will say. "I could see your confusion. I could feel your pain. But even in your darkest, most difficult hours, I saw a fierce little flame of love for Me deep in your spirit."

Your Edifying Words and Righteous Deeds

What are the milk, honey and fragrant garments the beloved mentions? Just as milk and honey help nurture bodies, the lips dripping with milk and honey are the bride's edifying, life-giving words that nurture the faith of the young instead of accusing, slandering, criticizing and faultfinding.

Her fragrant garments are her righteous deeds of service. The nineteenth chapter of Revelation describes the bride ready for the marriage to the Lamb. Of her garments it says:

> And it was given to her to clothe herself in fine linen, bright and clean; for the fine linen is the righteous acts of the saints (Rev. 19:8).

When the intention of our hearts is to be a servant, our service exudes a beautiful fragrance in the presence of God (2 Cor. 2:15-16). Our intent to lay our lives down for the Lord, crucifying our own self-centeredness, ascends like a pleasing perfume to the Lord.

Your Spirit Is Reserved for Him

Next, the beloved compares his bride to "a garden enclosed...a spring shut up, a fountain sealed" (Song 4:12, NKJV). Many of the gardens of the ancient world were open to all. Even animals could come and drink from their flowing springs and fountains. But the garden to which her beloved is referring is an enclosed, private garden reserved for the king.

A king's garden was a special place of pleasure and rest. It was not designed for economic productivity as a large field of grain would be. The king didn't count how many bushels of roses he harvested from his garden each year. No, he went to his garden to enjoy it, to be refreshed by its beauty.

In traveling in Europe I found the Hapsburg Palace in Vienna to be such a place. It has a magnificent garden which has been maintained over the years strictly for the pleasure of the king and his family. Completely walled-off from the rest of the palace, the garden is filled with tens of thousands of beautiful flowers.

The Lord is asking you and me to be His locked garden, His personal place of beauty and delight.

The heart of the bride was not open to the polluting spirit of the world. Her garden was locked up and sealed for only her beloved himself. She never left the gates standing ajar so strangers or animals could wander in. There was no "For Sale" sign posted. She continually said no to immorality, pride and greed. Her gifts and anointing were not to be sold or prostituted. They were used only for the pleasure of her beloved.

Submitting to His Dealings — Song of Solomon 4:16-5:1

As the beloved lavishes his love upon her, the bride breaks into one of the great prophetic cries of the Song of Solomon:

> Awake, O north wind,
> And come, wind of the south;
> Make my garden breathe out fragrance,
> Let its spices be wafted abroad.
> May my beloved come into his garden
> And eat its choice fruits (Song 4:16).

We know the north wind is the cold, bitter wind of winter, and the south wind is the warm, refreshing wind that comes during the sowing of the seed and the summer season of growth. The bride asks for both winds. She asks for the harsh north wind to blow on her in order to reveal what is in her heart, but she also asks for the blessing and refreshing of the south wind.

We never outgrow our need for the south winds of blessing. I've seen hyperspiritual people who thought they were more committed to God than He was to them. I've heard them pray, "Oh, God, forget the blessings. I just want the purging and purifying."

Let me tell you, I'm not even remotely tempted to tell God to forget the south winds. I love the blessings that flow in with the south winds. Normally I even reverse the order: "Send the south winds, God! Send the south winds! (And, oh, by the way, go ahead and send a few north winds, too.)" Unlike me, the bride had it in the right order. I'm still growing.

When we can ask for both winds — His dealings and His blessings — we are saying, "If You love me so much, I know it's safe to be Yours. I deeply trust You. I'm not afraid of difficult circumstances. You do not give anything that takes away real life. You have guarded my every step."

Don't confuse the north wind with the attack of the devil. We must always resist his onslaughts. We don't invite his attack. That's absolute foolishness, for we must always resist the devil and his dealings with us. But God can use the attacks of Satan to strengthen our hearts.

We can trust our Beloved absolutely. Therefore, we are not afraid to pray this prayer: "I love You, Jesus. I want all my immaturity to be gone. I want my heart to be yoked with Your heart. Your inheritance in me is the most important thing in my life. Therefore, awake, O north wind!"

The bride says, "Make *my* garden breathe out fragrance...May my beloved come into *his* garden and eat its choice fruits" (Song 4:16, italics added). She wants her beloved to get his full inheritance from her life. This is the prayer of the bondservant: "Come into every area of my heart, Lord. Eat with pleasure the fruit of my life."

Enduring the Rejection of Other Believers — Song of Solomon 5:6-8

Now comes the maiden's ultimate twofold test: Her beloved withholds his presence, and people reject her:

I opened to my beloved,
But my beloved had turned away and had gone!
My heart went out to him as he spoke.
I searched for him, but I did not find him;
I called him, but he did not answer me;
The watchmen who make the rounds in the city
    found me,
They struck me and wounded me;
The guardsmen of the walls took away my shawl
    from me.
I adjure you, O daughters of Jerusalem,
If you find my beloved,
As to what you will tell him:
For I am lovesick (Song 5:6-8).

This is the second time her beloved has left her. In chapter 3, he left in order to draw her into obedience. This time he has withdrawn his presence in order to test her.

Sooner or later, you and I will also confront this twofold test.

The first test is the loss of the conscious presence of God that so satisfies her soul. This is a temporary test. This withdrawing of God is not due to disobedience but rather because of her obedience and desire for full maturity.

It is as if the Lord is saying, "Let Me ask you, My bride: Am I only the source of your satisfaction, or am I the consuming goal of your life? Will you serve Me if there are no feelings? When My discernible presence is gone, will you say, 'I am Your loving bondservant. The issue is no longer that You are *my* inheritance. I am *Your* inheritance, my God, and I want You to receive the maximum good and glory from my life'?"

Step-by-step she is walking out her commitment to her beloved. He is no longer simply a stepping-stone to better things. He has become the magnificent obsession of her life.

While she is enduring the first test, suddenly it is time for the second, and it is equally severe. When we partake of

Christ's sufferings and abandon all to Him, we will endure the misunderstanding and rejection of other believers. This time the watchmen of the city find the maiden, strike and wound her, and take her covering.

Have fellow Christians — people to whom you have committed yourself — ever misunderstood you and risen up against you? For no justifiable reason, have they ever turned against you, wounded you and stripped you of your honor, place and function among other Christians? Do you know what it is to stand bleeding and naked, feeling as if God Himself has left you?

I do! I have had a group of pastors rise up against me with false stories and lies which reached across the nation. But even in that moment God told me to be quiet and bear it. If I would patiently wait for Him to act, He would reveal Himself to be even more precious than ever to me — and He did.

For a time, during the early, self-centered stages in our progression of holy passion we may seem to lose everything that initially drew us to Him. The wonderful spiritual feelings and awesome sense of His presence will sometimes be removed. It may appear that we have lost our inheritance in Him. Then when it seems as if we are stripped of those things through which we were able to bear fruit for our Beloved, it may also appear that He has lost His inheritance in us.

Like Job, this maiden did not know that the test she was experiencing would be only for a season. But in the midst of those feelings of pain and hurt, she was maturing. It is as if we can hear her proclaiming, "I'm not in it for myself anymore. I'm in it for you, my beloved. You are my passion and portion."

Next, we find her saying to the daughters of Jerusalem, whom I see as believers who are not yet awakened to fervency: "If you find my beloved, tell him I'm not angry. I'm not offended because he withdrew and let all this happen to me. I love him. I'm lovesick, not angry" (see Song 5:8).

When the Lord sees that beautiful response in us, even while we are walking in the midst of the fiery test, He exclaims, "Yes! Yes, that's the heart of My bride!"

The maiden's response attracts the attention of others. "What kind of beloved is your beloved, O most beautiful among women?" they ask (Song 5:9). To me, it is as if these daughters of Jerusalem, like Job's wife, are saying, "Why are you so tenaciously loyal to your beloved? After all, look what He has allowed to happen to you. Why not give up, curse God and die?" (see Job 2:9).

In my opinion, verses 10 through 16 of the fifth chapter of the Song of Solomon comprise the most outstanding statement of love in the Word of God. The maiden stands stripped and wounded before her accusers and answers, "My beloved is dazzling and ruddy, outstanding among ten thousand" (Song 5:10). The maiden then proceeds to describe some of the precious attributes of her beloved: his head, hair, eyes, cheeks, lips, hands, body, legs, countenance and mouth. She praises the excellence of who he is, the infinite loveliness of everything he does. "He's dazzling!...This is my beloved and this is my friend," she cries (Song 5:10,16).

She focuses on the reality of his majestic personality. It is the knowledge of her beloved that stabilizes her. She is overflowing in worship as she declares the splendor of his personhood through these ten attributes. Her response is not one of offense with him for withdrawing his presence and allowing rejection from others. Rather, she magnifies his greatness.

Bringing Others Into Intimacy With Him — Song of Solomon 6:3

What is the response of others when they see you and me standing utterly resolute in our commitment and unwavering in our affection for Jesus even in the midst of suffering, rejection and persecution? What is their response when they see that price is no object to us and that we are totally committed to Jesus regardless of what comes our way?

> Where has your beloved gone,
> O most beautiful among women?
> Where has your Beloved turned,
> That we may seek him with you? (Song 6:1).

Scoffers and accusers stop sneering, "Where is your Beloved now?" and start crying, "We want Him, too!"

As the Holy Spirit reveals more and more of the personality of Jesus to our hearts, our commitment will deepen, and an ever-increasing number of passionate believers will result. Some of these newly impassioned believers will be sixteen years old, some forty-five, some ninety-two. Some will be truck drivers and some chief executive officers of corporations. God is raising up a company of believers whose impassioned devotion to Him will inspire the rest of the body of Christ and prepare it for a great incoming harvest of souls.

What Can Subdue the Heart of God?

Like the beloved in the Song of Solomon, our Beloved sees when believers respond to the brutal tests of life with adoration and abandoned worship. He is utterly overwhelmed by His bride's devotion to Him:

> O my love, you are as beautiful as Tirzah,
> Lovely as Jerusalem,
> Awesome as an army with banners!
> Turn your eyes away from me,
> For they have overcome me (Song 6:4-5, NKJV).

"Turn your eyes away from me," our Beloved cries, *"for they have overcome me!"* Think of it! The God of heaven overwhelmed. No army, no principality, no power in heaven or earth can conquer Him who measured the waters in the hollow of His hand and marked off the heavens with the span of His fingers. The God who calculated the dust of the earth, weighed the mountains in a balance and the hills in a pair of scales. He who numbers the clouds and turns winter to spring. The God who calls all the stars by name. Only one thing can conquer God's heart: the affectionate love of His people who say yes to Him.

Continuing in the Progression of Holy Passion

We have seen in the beautiful Song of Songs that as our Beloved reveals the depths of His personality to us, that revelation enables us to stand firm in times of trouble and testing. As we begin to comprehend His majestic splendor and infinite loveliness, we are not offended when we do not understand the way He is leading us. Even in the most difficult, trying times our lips overflow with praise and adoration for our Beloved.

The Song of Solomon reveals some additional truths about the believer's passionate and affectionate relationship with her beloved. In Grace Training Center, our full-time leadership training program at Metro Vineyard, I teach many of these principles, including the following:

It asserts to us that after we have stood true to Jesus in the face of lying accusations and rejection, He Himself will validate us (6:4-13). We will no longer live for our pleasure, but for His pleasure alone (7:1-10).

As we labor with Him to reap the harvest, other believers across the nations of the world will come to love Jesus as we do (7:11–8:5). He will set the flaming seal of His love upon our hearts (8:6-7). The devotion and passion that Christ has for us will bring us to full maturity and overflowing passion for Him. Thus, He will receive His full inheritance from our lives (8:8-14).

Just as the glory of a man is his wife, we are the glory of

our Beloved as His bride, the one the Father gave Him from eternity past. We will rule and reign with Him. We will be His most prized possession!

The Song of Our Beloved

Let me encourage you to take the Song of Solomon and turn its verses into devotional meditation. This beautiful song of divine love is breathtaking when we begin to understand the prophetic nature of its words. They are life changing when we realize our Beloved is also speaking them over us, affirming and drawing forth qualities not yet fully developed in our lives. Oh, that God would give us new eyes to see His affectionate, yearning heart for us while we're still growing, still failing, still weak in so many ways.

Never allow the truths in God's beautiful love song to be forgotten and fade away in your heart. Cherish the message of His love for you. Jesus enjoys you and continually affirms you even in your imperfection and immaturity. Knowing He is enchanted with your beauty fills your heart with new courage and confidence. Understanding the affectionate personality of God equips you to wage war against the enemy and to demolish the lying, accusing strongholds he has erected in your mind. Resting in the sure and certain knowledge of God's ravished heart and overflowing, unwavering love will enable you to stand unoffended, unshaken and mature in times of trouble or persecution. Understanding that the powerful passions in the heart of God Himself are the source of holy passion in your own life ensures the continuing progression of your passion for Him.

As you have seen in the Song of Solomon, God pursues you with a relentless, infinite love. Do not let this truth grow cold in your heart. God is not some mystical, nebulous force that loves the masses but not individuals, whose love is focused on vast populations but not on a single person. You serve a deeply loving, passionate God whose heart is ravished by the beauty of your sincere, devoted heart. You are so beautiful to Him that you take His breath away!

I believe that in the years to come the Lord will release more revelation of Himself through the Song of Songs, the ravished song of the Beloved for His bride.

God, may You use the Song of Songs to release a thousand songs through a thousand languages. May Your message of love be sung fresh every time! May the revelation of Your ravished heart bring Your bride to full maturity.

TEN

The Knowledge of God
to the Ends of the Earth

In his book *Puritan Hope*[1] Iain Murray documents the coming of an end-times revival, giving biblical proof for the Puritan conviction that worldwide revival is set on God's schedule to occur before the return of the Lord.

A Worldwide Revival

Habakkuk prophesied this glorious revival: "The earth will be filled with the knowledge of the glory of the Lord, as the waters cover the sea" (Hab. 2:14).

Micah foretold it as well:

And He will arise and shepherd His flock
In the strength of the Lord,
In the majesty of the name of the Lord His God.
And they will remain,
Because at that time He will be great
To the ends of the earth (Mic. 5:4).

Not only will all peoples hear the great message of the gospel that Christ died for them. They will also see the demonstration of His great glory to the ends of the earth in the committed lives of people awakened to passion and fervency for God.

Paul's description of the glorious church is the clearest and most specific passage emphasizing this aspect of God's purpose for the church in the last days.

And He gave some as apostles, and some as prophets, and some as evangelists, and some as pastors and teachers, for the equipping of the saints for the work of service, to the building up of the body of Christ; *until* we all attain to the unity of the faith, and of the knowledge of the Son of God, to a mature man, to the measure of the stature which belongs to the fulness of Christ (Eph. 4:11-13, italics added).

When Paul says, "Attain to the...knowledge of the Son of God," he is not referring to the initial saving knowledge of the gospel. Paul is writing to the believers at Ephesus, assuring them that one of the purposes of the church's ministry is to lead people into an experiential knowledge of and intimacy with Jesus. These verses state very clearly that the church will attain to three specific things:

1. unity of faith

2. intimate knowledge of the splendor of Jesus

3. spiritual maturity

God's purposes with the church in this age are not complete until these three things take place: unity, intimacy and maturity.

The church will be restored to these three dimensions before the Lord comes back to take His bride unto Himself. God has been restoring various truths to the church for many years. I believe our generation is witnessing a new acceleration in God's activity of restoration. "Till we all come to the unity of the faith and the knowledge of the Son of God, to a perfect man, to the measure of the stature of the fullness of Christ" (Eph. 4:13, NKJV).

Some people are looking at Jerusalem, Israel, the temple or even at the Antichrist as they wait expectantly for the coming of the Lord. Or they look for the ten-nation confederacy or the European Common Market to determine the time of the Lord's coming. I believe the most important sign of the coming of the Lord is the restoration of the church to unity, intimacy and maturity.

Part of the church's restoration includes ministries that will function for the equipping and building up of the church into these three dimensions. Throughout church history and the common course of Christianity, we have seen some measure of these ministries wherever sincere people have been functioning in the body of Christ. But we are about to see them on a worldwide scale.

A New Measure of Zeal

How is the restoration of the church to come about? How will the redeemed be filled with the intimate knowledge of God and consumed with passionate affections for Him? "The zeal of the Lord of hosts will accomplish this" (Is. 9:7). In the coming decade I believe we will see a new measure of the zeal of the Lord of hosts. In the timing of the Father's perfect plan, the Holy Spirit will manifest His jealousy and zeal for Jesus in an unparalleled way, releasing blazing passion for the Son of God.

Restoring Jesus as the Focal Point of Redemption

The church has focused on many benefits of redemption — salvation, healing, wholeness, purity, power and authority. But we have not emphasized Jesus in His magnificent personhood as the focal point of redemption. The church knows Jesus redemptively as Savior but not intimately as an infinitely glorious person. The church has not experienced the excellencies of His divine perfections. In many ways Jesus is still a stranger in His own house. Yet the Word of God declares that an intimate understanding of Christ and His divine excellencies and perfections will fill the church (see Col. 2:2-3).

Jesus spoke with His disciples concerning His unique relationship with the Holy Spirit:

> If I do not go away, the Helper shall not come to you; but if I go, I will send Him to you...He shall glorify Me; for He shall take of Mine, and shall disclose it to you (John 16:7,14).

The Holy Spirit is released at Jesus' word, and He comes to this world with an agenda. At the very top of His list of divine activities and responsibilities is to glorify Jesus Christ by filling the people's affections with Jesus. How urgently the church needs that special ministry of the Holy Spirit.

Revealing Jesus to the Church

When Jesus Christ is revealed, a hunger for purity and

righteousness is released. What did Isaiah cry when he saw the Lord high and lifted up?

> Woe is me, for I am ruined!
> Because I am a man of unclean lips,
> And I live among a people of unclean lips;
> For my eyes have seen the King, the Lord of hosts
> (Is. 6:5).

Hunger for purity is one response of a believer who sees the Lord in His glory. Another response is being consumed with passion and zeal for Him, as Isaiah was when he cried, "Here am I. Send me!" (Is. 6:8).

Jesus isn't coming for a church that's gritting her teeth, struggling to stay free from sin, secretly wishing she could indulge in a little immorality but abstaining because of being afraid of getting caught. No, Jesus is coming for a church passionately and utterly devoted to Him — one that is free on the inside. The greatest motivation for obedience to the Lord is a growing revelation of who Jesus is — His passions and pleasures and the matchless splendor in His personality.

In Revelation 6:12-17, John describes the response of natural creation when the majestic, sovereign Jesus steps back into history again. There is a great earthquake. The sun becomes black as sackcloth. The moon becomes like blood. The stars of the sky fall to the earth. The sky is split apart like a scroll when it is rolled up. The mountains and islands are moved out of their places. All of mankind, from the greatest to the lowest, cry to the mountains and rocks, "Fall on us and hide us from the presence of Him who sits on the throne, and from the wrath of the Lamb; for the great day of their wrath has come; and who is able to stand?" (vv. 16-17). This universe will shake and reel because the King is stepping back into His creation to hold it accountable for its disobedience to Him.

Who is the Lord that you should honor and obey Him with

all of your time, money and talents? Who is the Lord that you should resist the pleasures, opportunities and positions that are outside His will for your life? Who is He that you should hunger and thirst for Him and set aside time to seek Him diligently? He is the magnificent King filled with infinite splendor and beauty. He is the Lord who possesses unlimited, majestic, sovereign power over all creation!

Preparing for the Coming Revival

So many Christians today are content to sit behind the church's stained-glass windows in their own little comfort zones, unconcerned with the disastrous plight of unbelievers outside the door of the church. Many believers are disillusioned and preoccupied with their own personal concerns, rather than being diligent in the prayer room for the needs of others.

I believe the charismatic church is in a mid-life crisis. Its members are content with just making a good life for themselves, with loving God and forgetting all else. Many believers are unwilling to take any new risks or to stretch beyond the known comfort of the church to take the love of God to those who know nothing of it.

Why are we Christians lolling around passively in our own little comfort zones, tuning out the Holy Spirit, neglecting the place of prayer and the Word of God? Why are we ignoring God's promptings to reach out to the lost and needy? Why do we compromise and backslide? What are we doing?

The Lord of indescribable splendor and glory is going to reveal Himself to the church. That revelation will awaken a deep response of absolute obedience and affection. We will never turn back to our compromise and passivity. The body of Christ will lay aside her shallow entertainment. She will have no need for the emptiness distracting her right now. She will reject the self-centered gospel she's been fed. She will lose her energy for strife, petty arguments and hurts.

I believe a great harvest of souls is coming. Tens of thousands will be added to the church in many of the major cities. God's people must be ready, since we are the ones who will be caring for the multitudes that come. History reveals that we will reproduce converts after our own kind. We will impart what we possess into those new believers.

I sometimes find myself praying, "God, don't fully release the harvest until You release something in Your church that is worthy of imparting to the multitudes of new converts. Don't allow another generation of easily offended Christians who lust for money, power, position and pleasure to be birthed. Please fill us with a more intimate knowledge of Your Son's splendor and loveliness before You bring a multitude of new believers for us to train — until we *all* attain to unity, intimacy and maturity."

The day of the spiritual superstar is over. God isn't interested in making men, ministries or churches famous. He's committed to spreading the fame of His Son throughout the nations. He's looking for believers who are ablaze with passion and devotion to His Son and will say, "I have only a moment on earth. My citizenship is in heaven, and I want to spread Your fame. I want to capture the hearts of the people for You!"

God ultimately desires to give His people greater grace and power. But I believe He will reserve the greater power — the mightier release of His Spirit — for the time when the church seeks to proclaim the riches of Christ's marvelous personality (Eph. 3:8). He will anoint and empower believers who seek to capture the hearts of others for His Son — not for themselves.

The Purpose of the Anointing

The Holy Spirit wants to impact people for Jesus, not for the latest exciting ministry in the nation or for the pastor with the biggest building. But strangely enough, the Holy Spirit does anoint men and women who do not glorify Jesus in their personal lives. He does it all the time.

As my ministry was first being formed in the mid-seventies, I'd look at some of the preachers and ask the Lord, "Why do You empower those evangelists who promote themselves so overtly?" As I began to grow in the Lord, I could almost sense the Holy Spirit cautioning me to imitate the Lord, not men, and to be sure of my own heart.

The church in the last days will have tenacious loyalty to the person of Jesus. If some of the ministries today have that loyalty, then imitate them. But if they don't, please don't be impressed just because some people fall down when the preacher prays for them. That's not enough. There's something greater than people falling down when we pray. I believe some of that may continue happening, but something more, something far better is on the horizon. We are about to discover what it means to live and minister in an overflow of our personal experience of the satisfying knowledge of the person of Christ.

One Abiding Purpose

Do you long to impact people for Jesus? Do you yearn to glorify Him in your personal life? Then I urge you to make the following verses two of the paramount prayers of your life.

Begin by praying "that the God of our Lord Jesus Christ, the Father of glory, may give to [me] a spirit of wisdom and of revelation in the knowledge of Him" (Eph. 1:17). Then take Christ's great prayer, "that the love wherewith Thou didst love Me may be in them" (John 17:26), and personalize it. Pray that you will love Jesus as God the Father loves Jesus.

Read those two verses over and over. Meditate on them. Write down what comes to your mind as you pray them. Begin asking God for a spirit of wisdom and revelation in the knowledge of Jesus' splendor and beauty. Ask that you might love the Son as the Father loves the Son. As God begins to answer those prayers, then you'll enjoy a life before the Lord that is holy and clean to the bone.

You and I must persevere until we are "strengthened with power through His Spirit in the inner man" (Eph. 3:16). We will be restless until we become prisoners of God. We will not experience true peace and fulfillment until He captures our love and obedience. As captives of His divine purpose, we will lead others unto passion for Jesus and into captivity to Him (Eph. 4:8).

I urge you to make being filled with the knowledge of the beauty and pleasures within God's personality your life vision. Lose yourself in the pursuit of knowing the passions and splendor of Christ Jesus. Proclaim His wonderful personality. Help others come to know and adore Him. Through the changing seasons of your life's ministry, and through the pruning of once fruitful activities and the budding forth of new ones, never allow that one abiding purpose to change.

The Generation of the Righteous

God isn't interested in elevating superstars so they can build their own personal kingdoms. He's interested in preparing a generation of righteous believers filled with the majestic splendor and indescribable loveliness of His Son. He is intent on answering the heart cries of those who yearn to be filled with passionate affections for His Son. He's interested in anointing a generation consumed with the desire to make His name known to the nations. It takes God's power to break and melt hard hearts. Let's look at one method that will help.

ELEVEN

The Blessings
of Intimacy

Some friends of mine remained childless after twenty-three years of marriage, much prayer, two major surgeries to correct infertility, endless rounds of testing and treatment and the expenditure of thousands of dollars. Refusing to be spiritually barren as well, the couple had decided long ago to invest their lives in the kingdom of God by ministering to others. The wife earned a doctorate so she could serve God more effectively in her calling. The husband, a successful businessman, became salt and light through the political offices he held in the metroplex where they lived.

Then God surprised them. A courageous young woman cancelled the abortion she had scheduled for the next day, carried her baby full-term and gave it up for adoption at birth, with the stipulation that the infant be placed in the home of a Christian couple who would rear the child for God. You guessed it. Through a series of divine coincidences and interventions, my friends, who hadn't even had their names on an adoption list because they were considered over the age limit to adopt, were blessed with a beautiful little boy just a few days old.

The elated couple understood that completing all the legal paperwork which established the baby's status as a member of their family was only a beginning. The greatest task lay ahead — establishing a deep, secure relationship of love between their adopted baby and themselves. They knew they would love their little son devotedly whether or not he ever returned their love, but they set out to win the child's love by demonstrating their love and affection for him. Bathed in an atmosphere of love, stability and lots of hugs and kisses, their son was a picture of contentment and security.

Time passed, and one afternoon as the couple drove up in front of their lovely home, their little boy exclaimed, "*My* house!" It was indeed. Everything that hard-working father and mother owned had been willed to him from the moment he'd become a member of their family. All they had was his.

Then the day came when the couple's little son began to return their affection. His father kissed him on the cheek and whispered, "I love you," just as he'd done a thousand times before. The little boy looked up, smiled and said, "I you!" As the "I you" eventually expanded to "I love you," juicy kisses and countless hugs, that father felt something of what God must feel when His children begin passing beyond the stage of self-centered receiving and start returning love to Him.

Can we ever hope to comprehend the depth of love God has demonstrated for us by making us sons and daughters in His own house? As J. I. Packer writes in his book *Knowing God*, "The New Testament gives us two yardsticks for measuring God's love. The first is the cross (1 John 4:8-10); the second is the gift of sonship (1 John 3:1). Of all the gifts of grace, adoption is the highest."[1]

God the Father adopted you and me as His children, gave Himself to us as our loving Father and made us fellow heirs with Jesus because He chose to, not because He had to.

The Motive for Spiritual Growth

What best motivates a child to want to be like his parents? Is it intimacy, love and respect, or isolation, fear and guilt? The same principle is true in the spiritual realm. Using wrong motivations to encourage believers to pursue intimacy with Christ — fear, force, guilt trips or manipulation — may seem to obtain quick results, but those results won't last. Even spiritual disciplines such as prayer, fasting, Bible study and witnessing often result in legalism, pride, insecurity or morbid introspection if pursued with the wrong motivation.

Christians will sometimes move into action faster if they are told God is angry and losing interest in them; or that they're going to fail miserably, losing everything that's dear to them on earth if they don't get busy performing and producing. However, in the long run, some very sincere believers will wind up damaged, discouraged and burned out because they've built their spiritual lives on faulty foundations.

The heart knowledge of God's deep affection and full acceptance for you and me as His own beloved children is the best motivation for consistent spiritual growth. As Paul explained to the Roman believers, "You have not received a spirit of slavery leading to fear again, but you have received a spirit of adoption as sons by which we cry out, 'Abba! Father!' " (Rom. 8:15). Our spirits cry and long for more of Him when we see His loving adoption of us as His children, rather than condemnation.

Being rooted and grounded in the strong, secure love of God motivates us to greater consistency, spiritual passion and maturity. As we begin to understand the Father's affection and the price Jesus paid to redeem us, our hearts melt with devotion and gratitude. We long for a fuller, more intimate knowledge of God and for heart-to-heart fellowship with Him. We desire to become wise children who bring joy to our Father. Instead of becoming prodigal sons or the "black sheep" of His family, we want to "hang out" with Jesus, our elder brother, and grow up to be just like Him.

As you and I pursue intimacy with Jesus, it will become apparent that we are God's royal children. *We will manifest our family's likeness* by conforming to Christ. *We will seek to further our family's welfare* by loving our brethren. *We will maintain our family's honor* by avoiding what our Father hates, pursuing what He loves and seeking His glory. As we cultivate intimacy with Jesus, out of the riches of His glory we will be "strengthened with power through His Spirit in the inner man" (Eph. 3:16).

Seven Blessings of Holy Passion

The first step toward experiencing intimacy with Jesus is our decision to pursue *Him* more than we pursue other good things such as anointing, happiness and success. When you set your heart to seek the Lord, your life will begin to change in many ways. Here are a few:

1. A Focus on Intimacy Washes Our Spirits.

Jesus loved the church and gave Himself up for her "that He might sanctify her, having cleansed her by the washing of water with the word, that He might present to Himself the church" in glorious splendor (Eph. 5:26-27).

Just as you or I need a daily physical bath, we also need a daily spiritual bath to remove some of the "grime" and defilement. If it is allowed to accumulate, it will lead to spiritual dullness and insensitivity in our spirits. Inner corruption such as anger, slander, impatience and sensuality grieves the Holy Spirit and makes our spirits insensitive and unable to respond fully to Him.

When we fix our hearts on the *person* of Jesus and dialogue with Him, the Word of God washes our spirits. Defilement from our daily contact with a fallen world is cleansed away. The accumulation of information about the Scriptures and the mental discipline of hours of Bible study will never thoroughly cleanse the inner man in the way that devotional, worshipful meditation upon God's Word will. In Bible study alone, we store up important scriptural facts and concepts. But when our Bible study leads into personal dialogue with Jesus as we meditate upon His cleansing Word, we also experience growth in spiritual hunger, sensitivity and nearness to Him.

2. A Focus on Intimacy Protects Our Souls.

We will never possess true purity without inward affection for Jesus. External disciplines and standards of holiness without devotion for Jesus have very little real power or life in them. A person named Jesus — not rules and regulations — guards our souls. Affection for Him creates a hindrance to the added temptations plaguing our souls. Let me share one practical example.

When passion for Jesus is built into our spiritual foundations, this resolution in our spirits automatically repels the sensual communications others send us. It returns the message "No, I'm not available." That strong, clear message rises from within our spirits, nipping temptation in the bud.

We are filled with such longings and affections for Jesus

that we refuse to become involved in sensuality and wrong relationships. It's not a matter of being afraid we might get caught. It's not an issue of fear that we might be shamed and lose honor, position, privileges or even the anointing. We have higher motives for resisting temptation than a fear of AIDS or of coming under divine discipline. Our hearts are shielded by our love and reverence for Christ.

One of the greatest glories of Christ's church is her cleanliness, her purity. The believer deeply in love with Jesus — the soul aggressively engaged in pursuing intimacy with Him — is positioned to overcome temptation. This is true even in natural relationships. Not very many people are tempted to become romantically involved with someone other than their new spouse while on their honeymoon. Most newlyweds are so aware of the love they share with one another, the temptation to have an affair with someone else seems absurd. On the other hand, the passive soul wandering from fantasy to fantasy and lacking affection for God is vulnerable to almost any temptation that happens along.

In our pursuit of intimacy with Jesus, you and I must realize that feelings will come and go, swinging from holy passion to spiritual barrenness. We will have seasons of deep, fervent, longing love for Jesus, when we pray with great feelings of inspiration. But we will also experience seasons when we pray without any feeling of God's presence. Yet, as we persist, we will begin to realize that even in the dry, barren seasons our hearts are growing more fervent in mature love toward Jesus. Our focus is on Jesus, not upon feelings which seem to have fled forever.

As Paul declares, "The greatest of these is love" (1 Cor. 13:13). Love is our greatest motive. It is our greatest strength, joy, protection and perseverance. The breastplate of Christ's love for us and our love for Him is the greatest piece of our spiritual armor. Only foolish presumption dares enter into spiritual warfare without it.

3. A Focus on Intimacy Motivates and Inflames Our Hearts.

When we are "sowing to the Spirit" (Gal. 6:8), we are exposing ourselves to the presence of God whether we feel it or not. As focusing upon Him becomes the habit of our souls, we receive the wonderful anointing spoken of in Hebrews, "Who makes His...ministers a flame of fire" (1:7). The flaming heart of Christ ignites our hearts. Fire begets fire.

I love the verse from the Song of Solomon where the beloved speaks to his bride and says,

> Put me like a seal over your heart,
> Like a seal on your arm.
> For love is as strong as death,
> Jealousy is as severe as Sheol;
> Its flashes are flashes of fire,
> The very flame of the Lord (Song 8:6).

The holy flame is relentless and consuming. It will ignite a focused soul, even though it may be barren, and release deep emotions of hunger for Jesus. However, if we are too busy, easily offended, bitter or self-absorbed, the flame will be diminished.

It's important that we understand this principle: While it is true that a Christian's careless living will cause the flame to die down, this does not mean God's *love* has decreased toward that believer. You and I must refuse to believe the subtle lie of the enemy that says God's love for us goes up and down with our own vacillating spiritual feelings and attainments. The flame we're talking about here doesn't represent God's love and affections for us: It represents our passion and zeal for Him. We can lose our passion for Jesus without losing God's love for us.

4. A Focus on Intimacy Satisfies Our Human Spirits.

Intimacy satisfies the deep longing in our spirits. People

who are born again are not always filled with a sense of the nearness of God. Effective ministry produces a satisfaction that comes through helping others and being useful in God's kingdom, but it is not a permanent, deep satisfaction. Nothing but an intimate relationship with Jesus will satisfy this inner cry birthed by the Holy Spirit.

The Holy Spirit may give spiritual gifts to believers and release the benefits of redemption upon us, but none of those things will ultimately satisfy the desire in our spirits for Jesus Himself. When our spiritual hunger is not being satisfied, you and I will experience frustrating boredom and holy restlessness. The Spirit of God is trying to stir up our spirits to seek more of God.

5. A Focus on Intimacy Frees Us From Insecurity and Fear of Man.

Intimacy with Jesus brings a deepened security and rest in the inner man. As we interact in a deeply personal way with Him, we grow in our knowledge that we are accepted and cherished by God. This knowledge progressively frees us from feelings of insecurity and the intimidating, paralyzing fear of others' opinions or actions against us.

A focus on Jesus ultimately leads us to the knowledge of His heart of affirmation. This is absolutely vital. As important as human affirmation is, it is woefully inadequate without God's affirmation of us. It is the knowledge that we are loved, accepted and valued by God that gives us a sense of value and true self-worth. When we are secure and confident in God's love, we grow out of our fears. When we know we are pleasing Him, criticism and offenses from others won't affect us as easily. "Proving" our value to others ceases to be the dominant drive in our emotional makeup. God's pleasure and His approving smile are all we need.

6. *A Focus on Intimacy Heals Inner Wounds of the Heart.*

I believe that counseling is a part of the process of emotional healing. Like almost everything God restores to the church, counseling and inner healing have been abused and taken to extremes in some cases. But that doesn't mean these ministry tools should be shunned. The cure for abuse is *proper* use, not *dis*use. However, if a person's wounded heart is to experience true, lasting wholeness and healing, that individual needs to be introduced to the Healer Himself and encouraged to build a relationship of intimacy with Him.

Human hearts can be wounded in many ways. Almost daily we hear another tragic story of sexual, physical, verbal or emotional abuse. Victims range in age from tiny infants to the elderly. Man's inhumanity to man seems to defy all limits. Yet, when I think about this subject of healing inner wounds of the heart, I can't help but think of my brother, Pat. Few human hearts have been dealt harder blows than Pat's heart suffered after becoming a quadriplegic at the age of seventeen. Then he lost the most precious person in the world to him only eight months later when Dad died.

I watched Pat fight an enemy that could be worse than paralysis or death, and I saw him win. My brother refused to allow bitterness to conquer him. I can tell you this: My brother is a champion of courage.

He is still paralyzed from the neck down. But my brother's spirit is now unhindered by weights of self-pity, hatred or bitterness. For many years now, Pat has loved Jesus with a passion. Over the years he has been a man of prayer, bearing the burdens of others and lifting their needs up to God. Watching my brother's example has affirmed to me many, many times that an intimate relationship with Jesus can heal *any* wound of the human heart.

How are the inner wounds of the heart healed? We have to give everything to God, including our bitterness, self-pity and desire for revenge. Our grief, anger, shame and pride — even our hopes, dreams and ambitions — must be laid on God's altar, along with our personal rights and the desire to run our own lives. Jesus Christ must become the focus of our hearts — not our tragedies, our past or all that might have been. Only Jesus can transform self-pity into praise or tears into triumph. A focus on intimacy with Jesus heals the inner wounds of the heart. My brother's life daily affirms that fact.

7. *A Focus on Intimacy Is an Effective Means of Spiritual Warfare.*

The strength of spiritual warfare is passion for Jesus. The enemy's strategy is to shift us from an offensive mode into a defensive mode where we're attempting to ward off temptation and sin through the power of our own wills and resolution. He fears offensive Christianity that pursues the person of Christ and fills our lives with purpose. If Satan can separate us from our passion and from our purpose, then we become passive and aimless — an easy prey for sin.

Let's look at two scriptural principles illustrating the wisdom of maintaining an offensive posture when dealing with the enemy: The principle of increasing and decreasing and the principle of light and darkness.

The Principle of Increasing and Decreasing

"He must increase, but I must decrease" (John 3:30). This principle can be applied outside of its original context where John was allowing Jesus' ministry to replace his own. It also applies to how we grow as individuals.

Increase in our knowledge of God comes before decrease in our bondage to darkness. That's God's divine order. Trying to decrease in sin when Jesus has not first increased in us is difficult and ineffective. Once the knowledge of God's personality penetrates our human spirits, it has a sanctifying impact on our emotions. As Jesus becomes more real to us, the inevitable result is a desire to give ourselves to Him and to decrease those things in our lives that are working in opposition to Him.

The Principle of Light and Darkness

Believers combat spiritual darkness in their lives with spiritual light! John speaks of Jesus in terms of light: "In Him was life, and the life was the light of men" (John 1:4). John continues, "And the light shines in the darkness, and the darkness did not comprehend it." Darkness is driven out of the human spirit by the light of the revelation of Jesus Christ through the Word of God. No darkness in the life of a sincere believer has the force to overpower His light.

Attempting to drive the darkness out of our hearts by ourselves is frustrating and futile, but when the person of Christ is unveiled to us, and His light enters our hearts, the darkness flees. The same is true of natural light in a room, for the darkness in a room disappears when we turn on the light. We can't empty out the darkness to make room for light. Rather, we allow the light to enter, and darkness is automatically overpowered. We wear ourselves out by trying to prepare and make way for more light by focusing on trying to drive out the darkness. Instead, we should indirectly attack the darkness in our lives by focusing on the release of more light.

Satan is not intimidated by the shouts and boasts of believers who do not have an intimate relationship with Jesus. He knows that as long as darkness reigns unchallenged and unconquered in many areas of their own lives, those believers pose no real threat to his kingdom. Jesus is the One whom Satan fears. If believers are not filled with the reality and knowledge of Christ, Satan knows it is only a matter of time until they will become victims, not victors.

Satan is troubled by believers who are undistracted from the purity and simplicity of devotion to Jesus. He flees before the sword of the Spirit when it is wielded by men and women who have a history of faithfulness and obedience through their intimacy with God. He is hindered through the prayers of godly intercessors that pierce the darkness, exposing and destroying his strongholds (2 Cor. 10:5).

Isaiah declares, "Neither has the eye seen a God besides Thee, who acts in behalf of the one who waits for Him" (64:4). No matter how weak, imperfect and immature we are, if we will set ourselves to seek God's face and wait upon Him, continuing to persevere in prayer, God's mighty hand will move on our behalf. Divine acts are loosed even in response to weak humans who wait upon the Lord.

A focus on intimacy is an effective means of spiritual warfare, for Satan is hindered by passion for Jesus, purity and persevering prayer. The weakest, most immature believer who has a heart focus of holy passion will become a threat to Satan's kingdom.

Invited to Intimacy

As we continue to focus on intimacy with Jesus, we will be rewarded and enriched by the release of these seven supernatural benefits in our lives. Let's review them once more.

1. Our spirits will be washed from defilement by the Word of God.

2. Our souls will be strengthened against temptation by the breastplate of faith and love affecting our emotions.

3. Our inner man will be motivated and inflamed by a release of divine hunger and zeal as our spirits are exposed to Jesus' flaming heart.

4. The deep cry in our spirits for intimacy with Jesus will be satisfied.

5. We will be freed from insecurity and the fear of man.

6. Inner wounds of the heart will be healed.

7. We will be equipped for spiritual warfare.

The choices are clear-cut: Passion or passivity? Victor or victim? Blessings or barrenness?

You and I are invited to pursue a person actively, for intimacy does not come accidentally. Intimacy comes through the hunger and yearning of our hearts and through sowing to the Spirit. As we hunger and thirst for Jesus, seeking Him and spending time in His presence, we will fall in love with Him.

TWELVE

Gazing on the Throne of God

I can picture it now: the moment in eternity thousands of earth years from now when one redeemed saint turns to another and says, "Remember the earthly days when we battled sensuality, greed and pride? When our souls were continually vexed by the lust of that present world?"

"Yes, I remember all right. How we could have allowed such temporal desires to drive us away from God is hard to imagine. All of us from Adam's race, from the very first generation to the very last, invested and built our lives around unholy desires and pleasures that endured only a fleeting moment."

"It seems so absurd in retrospect, doesn't it? What were we doing, loving the passing pleasures of a fallen age? What were we thinking, investing our emotions in empty cravings, selling our souls for money and continually struggling to promote ourselves?

"Face it. The god of that world did his work well, blinding so many of us to the real issues and thereby obscuring the eternal realities. Sin always has been a bankrupt system, and we had not the sense to know it. If we'd only taken the wisdom and truth found in the Lord's book, we would have seen the warning of the holy One: 'The world is passing away, and also its lusts; but the one who does the will of God abides forever' " (1 John 2:17).

Do you think the idea of conversations in heaven about our life on earth is far-fetched? I don't think it will be too surprising if we hear many such discussions in eternity.

One of the reasons I love the book of Revelation is that it keeps our time and purpose here on earth in clear perspective. It displays such striking contrasts: heaven and earth, time and eternity, evil and good, illusion and reality, lies and truth, the kingdom of light and the kingdom of darkness. Reading the book of Revelation is a powerful reminder that this world is passing away. It sets our focus on the world that is to come, instead of on Wall Street. It reminds us of an eternal throne in the heavens. It reveals the majesty and eternity of Him who sits on that throne and the indescribable splendor of the glorious person who is seated at His right hand. Revelation 1:3 even promises a blessing upon those who read the book, open their hearts to the things written in it and seek to heed them.

Gazing on the Throne of God

In the past when I prayed I felt as though I were praying into the air — to some nebulous being, far beyond the grasp of my realities. I had a feeling of disconnectedness, with no real sense of praying to a real person.

But my prayer life has been transformed and enriched through a simple devotional aid I discovered some years ago I call it "gazing on God's throne."

John describes the scene in heaven into which our prayers ascend. He tells us what happens when we lift our voices and say, "Father, I love You." He paints a word picture of the setting to which our requests and petitions come. It was this description of God's throne, the Lord Jesus, the four living creatures and twenty-four elders that significantly changed my prayer life.

As Tozer said, "We must practice the art of long and loving meditation upon the majesty of God,"[1] that is, a reverent meditation on the being of God. I took his counsel and began meditating upon the majesty of God. That's when the fourth chapter of Revelation opened up to me.

To aid my meditation, I studied Revelation 4 phrase by phrase, using the Bible itself as my commentary. Especially in the writings of Daniel and Ezekiel I found similar word pictures that made the scene John described even more vivid (see Dan. 7:9,10,13; Ezek. 1; Matt. 19:28; 1 Kin. 22:19; Rev. 5; 15:2; 20:4; Phil. 2:5-11). As I continued my study, the person of God, heaven's throne room and what happens there when we pray and worship and sing praises to God became more and more real to me.

It's not some counterfeit New Age visualization technique. Picturing the awesome scene John describes in the fourth chapter of Revelation helps me enjoy holy fellowship with Jesus. Instead of "praying into the air," I often focus my thoughts upon the loving, majestic person seated upon His glorious throne and speak into His heart.

In Revelation 4:1 John says, "After these things I looked, and behold, a door standing open in heaven" (NKJV). In a vision the aged apostle was able to gaze directly into the heart of heaven's throne room. Read his awesome, eye-witness account:

Immediately I was in the Spirit; and behold, a
throne set in heaven, and One sat on the throne.
And He who sat there was like a jasper and a
sardius stone in appearance; and there was a rainbow around the throne, in appearance like an emerald. Around the throne were twenty-four thrones,
and on the thrones I saw twenty-four elders sitting,
clothed in white robes; and they had crowns of gold
on their heads. And from the throne proceeded
lightnings, thunderings, and voices. Seven lamps of
fire were burning before the throne, which are the
seven Spirits of God. Before the throne there was a
sea of glass, like crystal. And in the midst of the
throne, and around the throne, were four living
creatures...The four living creatures, each having six
wings, were full of eyes around and within. And
they do not rest day or night, saying:

"Holy, holy, holy,
Lord God Almighty,
Who was and is and is to come!" (vv. 2-
6,8, NKJV).

Here is a picture of the throne of grace (Heb. 4:16). It is
not a throne of legalism or religion. God has invited all of His
people to come before this throne that they might receive
mercy and find grace to help them in their time of need. But
it is much more than that.

This throne is an eternal reality. It won't become real when
we get to heaven and see it for the first time — it is real now.
It doesn't exist just because we are in need, for it has existed
from eternity past. It was secured in eternity before the
heavens and earth were ever created.

Jesus Christ's finished work on the cross has made it possible for weak, broken people to come freely before this
throne, with no condemnation.

God the Father raised Christ from the dead, seated Him at His right hand in the heavenly places, put all things in subjection under His feet and gave Him as head over all things to the church, which is His body (Eph. 1:20-23). The Lord Jesus is able to save forever those who draw near to God through Him, since He always lives to make intercession for them (Heb. 7:25).

The Spirit of God is constantly beckoning the saints on earth to live before the throne. One day we will joyfully cast our crowns before this throne. These crowns represent our spiritual achievements as we walked before the Lord in obedience and cooperated with the gracious work of the Holy Spirit in our lives (Rev. 4:10). But first we need to learn to cast our hearts before it in devotion and passion for the Son of God.

Finding Meaning for Our Lives

This throne, filled with the grace of God, is the most awesome place in all existence. It is the foundation of the entire created order. It is the center of everything. It is the purpose for everything, for He who created all things sits upon the throne, and all things exist for His pleasure (Rev. 4:11).

When we stand before Him at the judgment seat, what He is thinking about us will be the only thing that counts. Once I understood that the only thing relevant to my life is what God thinks is relevant, then I had a clearer grasp of the meaning of my life.

Our lives only have meaning as we understand them with respect to obedience to Christ Jesus who is seated at the Father's right hand. If we lose our focus on Him, then we lose our connection with reality, purpose and order. If we lose our vision of the throne of God as the center of everything we live for, then we lose our equilibrium and stability. We lose our reason for enduring hardships. We lose our motivation to bless our enemies. We lose the real reason why God gives us good things.

When we lose the awareness of God our Father on this throne with Jesus seated at His right hand, then our problems become insurmountable in our thinking. The despair can be unbelievable. We forget that everything else passes away, and nothing has any significance, relevance and meaning outside the reality of the person upon this throne. All else is temporal, except the things that are pleasing to Him.

The Family of God

Notice how the angels and the twenty-four elders address God. They refer to Him as "Lord God Almighty, who was and is and is to come!" (Rev. 4:8, NKJV); "Him who sits on the throne"; and "Him who lives forever and ever" (Rev. 5:13,14, NKJV).

But Jesus taught us to address Him as "Father": "In this manner, therefore, pray: Our Father..." (Matt. 6:9, NKJV).

And Paul reminded us that we have received a spirit of adoption as sons by which we cry out, "Abba, Father" (Rom. 8:15, NKJV).

The angelic host does not call Him "our Father." Only Jesus and born-again believers — the adopted sons and daughters of God who have entered into the blessed Father-child relationship with God solely on the grounds of Christ's sonship — have the privilege of calling Him "Abba, Father" which translates, "Daddy, Daddy."

A Worshipping Community

Jesus said to pray that His will would be done on earth as it is in heaven (Matt. 6:10). The community of God on earth — the church, the Father's family — is part of a larger community already in heaven. The community of God on earth is to live as the community of God lives in heaven.

The community of God in heaven is filled with worship and adoration for Him. They recognize and gaze upon the greatness, beauty, loveliness and splendor of Jesus on His throne. They deeply love the Son of God. They gaze upon Him at the throne of grace. The church on earth is also to be a passionate, worshipping community existing to give ourselves wholly to the Son of God. The purpose of both God's community in heaven and God's community on earth begins and ends with worship around the throne.

It is a sad fact that many Christians rarely come before the throne. This does not mean that these believers are spiritual failures. It does not mean that they are uninterested in or indifferent to God. Many sincere believers long for a more satisfying relationship with God and are eager to experience His presence. But it means that their lives are not being enriched by the grace of God coming from the throne. Instead of living in contact with the awesome One seated upon the throne, many in the body of Christ are neglecting and disregarding this sacred privilege.

Some believers focus on the throne of God, contemplating His glory and majesty, for a few short minutes during the worship time on Sunday morning. But many Christians are unaware that God longs for us to experience a taste of the worship before His throne now — before we get to heaven. Consequently, today's church bears painful wounds and ugly scars that are the results of our ignorance and negligence.

The believing community doesn't function properly when we neglect to touch God's heart, therefore losing our intimate communion with Him.

If I am enjoying the Lord, I can feel mistreated by others, and it doesn't bother me. But if I am not enjoying the intimacy of His presence, I am more easily irritated. When that happens, I get off in a quiet place for a few hours and immerse myself in such classics as Tozer, the Puritan writings or even the Song of Solomon. That practice is like a medicine, refreshing me and making me happy. Whatever was bothering me is not a burden anymore.

Without the person of the Lord Jesus as its central focus, without enjoying the Lord and having tenderized hearts, the church cannot function as a dynamic community serving one another in deep fellowship. Strife and division result when believers attempt to draw close to one another without also drawing close to Jesus. The only way God's community on earth can function according to design is for Christ to be the center. However, if you and I lose that focus, our brokenness can be healed if we will come in prayer to God's throne of grace and cast our hearts before Him.

In his vision, John the apostle describes four living creatures and twenty-four elders falling down before the Lord Jesus, the Lamb of God, "each having a harp, and golden bowls full of incense, which are the prayers of the saints" (Rev. 5:8, NKJV). I believe that the harps speak symbolically of our worship, and the fragrant incense refers to our prayers ascending before God's throne in the midst of myriads of angels.

A description is given of worshipping believers standing on the sea of glass that is mingled with fire (Rev. 15:2). We speak into God's heart as He joyfully hears us from His throne.

I began to realize that, when we pray, God does not want us speaking lightly and nonchalantly into the air as if to no one. He wants us speaking into His heart. Therefore, as I prayed, I talked to a real, glorious person, offering my praise, worship, prayers and self directly to Him. I'd picture myself standing on that sea of glass filled with fire as I gazed on the throne surrounded by the rainbow. When I did, my thoughts and feelings changed.

My problems did not suddenly disappear, but the way I thought and felt about them changed into a more proper, balanced perspective. I discovered that the songwriter had been right after all: The things of earth really do grow strangely dim in the light of His glory and grace.[2]

In the two decades that have transpired since that time, I have continued this practice of gazing on the throne and communing intimately with an awesome, infinitely lovely, gracious person.

Since we are seated in heavenly places with Christ (Eph. 2:6), learning to speak directly into the heart of a real, glorious person seated on His throne in the heavens is one of the essential dynamics of inspiring devotional prayer.

In seeking to help others grow in their prayer lives, I've been teaching and leading prayer meetings regularly for over fifteen years. Nearly every day for ten years I led prayer meetings in our church body, and for almost five of those years three times a day — morning, afternoon and evening.

In these meetings I sometimes give a short instructional message and model a prayer for those attending. Then several persons from my leadership team may also pray, following the model I have just taught.

An average of twenty to thirty different people will come to each meeting. In fact, I encourage everyone in the church to go at least once a week.

In the last four years when I've been at home, I have still led three prayer meetings a day several times a week. And while I'm traveling I teach on personal devotional prayer and corporate intercessory prayer for revival.

This emphasis on prayer is something the Lord has mandated for us as a church body. But because of it, we have become deficient in other ministries. We are now emphasizing small groups for pastoral care and evangelism, and we're noticing a decline in attendance at prayer meetings. And that's OK. When an increase comes in one area, a decrease is inevitable in another area.

Many people have told me over the years that, by being challenged to know the personality of God and to have a fervent heart for Him, passion has awakened in their hearts. Even people with the dullest of hearts have been impacted.

My prayer is that more and more pastors will preach this

message and that more members of the body of Christ will open themselves up to it.

For the last twenty years I have deliberately opened up my own heart by listening to tapes and reading books by people who emphasize this message. Years ago a preacher on a tape challenged me to read *The Life of David Brainerd* by Jonathan Edwards. Edwards was a well-known theologian living in the 1700s in America. Brainerd served as a missionary to the American Indians in the 1740s. The book turned out to be the single most influential book I've ever read outside the Bible.

Books on the attributes and personality of God, such as those by A. W. Tozer, A. W. Pink and J. I. Packer, the works of Jonathan Edwards and devotional classics by the Puritans may help to awaken passion in your heart.

Heaven's Throne Room

We are seated in heavenly places with Christ (Eph. 2:6). Do you ever imagine standing in heaven's throne room as you worship and intercede? Sometimes I whisper, "Oh, how I love You, Lord. Give me insight into Your glorious throne." Then, without saying a word, I simply gaze into the awesome scene that John the apostle and other holy men of old have described for us.

Look with me at the astounding glimpse the Word of God gives us into this invisible world that rules our visible world. Picture a mighty throne, immersed in flames, standing in heaven. Imagine an indescribably glorious person with hair like pure wool and garments as white as snow, seated upon that throne. His appearance is like the shining, dazzling brightness of light green jasper and fiery red sardius. Picture a bright arch that looks like a rainbow of emerald encircling the entire throne. This radiance about Him, like the appearance of a rainbow in the clouds, is the appearance of the likeness of the glory of the Lord.

Watch the flashes of lightning and listen to the rumblings and peals of thunder coming out from the throne. Gaze in awe at the flowing river of fire before Him. Picture twenty-four lesser thrones surrounding the great thrones on the right and the left and twenty-four elders clothed in white and wearing golden crowns sitting upon those thrones.

In front of the throne of Him who lives forever throughout eternity, imagine the flames of seven blazing torches — the sevenfold Spirit of God — reflected in an immense sea of transparent glass like crystal, mixed with fire. The awesome, dazzling expanse of this clear, glassy sea mirrors the entire scene, creating a mirror image.

Daniel 7:9-10 describes a river of fire flowing from His throne presumably into the sea of glass that is mingled with fire (Rev. 15:2). Picture four, six-winged, living beings hovering around the blazing throne. They are full of eyes in front and behind, signifying intelligence as to what is before and behind them. Listen as day and night these beings never cease to proclaim passionately, "Holy, holy, holy, Lord God Almighty, who was and is and is to come!" (Rev. 4:8, NKJV).

Music! Do you hear the music? Let your soul drink in every note as the twenty-four elders strum their harps and sing a glorious song of worship to Jesus, the Lamb of God. Listen to the mighty roar of praise ascending from the myriads and myriads of angels on every side of the throne as together they cry out, extolling the Lamb who was sacrificed for us.

Look! Do you see Him? Jesus is there at the right hand of His Father. His loveliness and His splendor are beyond description. He is welcoming you to the throne of grace, smiling and bidding you to come. The mighty throngs of angels are parting to let you through, for they step aside softly when they see a child of God approaching.

Revelation 15:2 describes the place where we stand on the sea of glass mingled with fire. We stand here as we speak into His heart.

That is the scene into which I come to offer my devotional prayers. And you can enter that scene in your prayer life also.

As we come there, day after day, year after year, our lives are enriched; our spirits are invigorated; and our minds are renewed. We are cleansed from the defilements of earth, and our souls are restored. The fruitless, temporal things of earth lose their hold upon us as we behold them from the perspective of that eternal, invisible world. And over the course of time we are changed — transformed — from glory to glory.

The Fivefold Response

John describes five specific actions being carried out by the four living creatures and twenty-four elders in response to the person seated on the throne:

> Whenever the living creatures give *glory* and *honor* and *thanks* to Him who sits on the throne, who lives forever and ever, the twenty-four elders fall down before Him who sits on the throne and *worship* Him who lives forever and ever, and *cast their crowns* before the throne, saying:
>
> > You are worthy, O Lord,
> > To receive glory and honor and power;
> > for You created all things,
> > And by Your will they exist, and were created (Rev. 4:9-11, italics added, NKJV).

Notice the awesome activity taking place around the throne of God. The four living creatures are giving God glory, honor and thanks. The twenty-four elders are giving Him worship and casting their crowns before Him.

I don't claim to have captured the complete definition of any of these words and phrases. But I believe we need to take time to consider five responses flowing out of the hearts of the living creatures and the elders as they worship before God on His throne. Reflect upon the corresponding implications of these five responses for you and me as believers today.

1. *Giving Glory to God*

First, the four living creatures are continually giving glory to God. What does it mean to "give God glory"? How can you and I give Him glory? Paul said we "glory in Christ Jesus" — we joy and delight in the glorious personhood of Jesus (Phil. 3:3). When we give God glory, we express passionate adoration holy affections filled with desire for God.

I believe the Lord is showing me that He is going to give a gift to the church, both in the United States and worldwide. I see it happening in books, seminars and leadership conferences around the world.

In the coming years, He is going to raise up leaders who know His personality from experiencing Him in their own lives. Men and women who are filled with extravagant affection for Jesus will emerge and rise to places of leadership. Like Paul, they also will "glory in Christ Jesus." They will proclaim the Word of God and lead other believers into passionate affections for the Son of God. God is going to be given glory by a church filled with holy affections for Him.

2. *Giving God Honor*

> Although they knew God, they did not glorify Him as God (Rom. 1:21, NKJV).

What does it mean to give God honor? We honor Him with our reverence and praise. We also honor God through a life of radical obedience that backs up our desires to glorify Him with a heart of holy affections. This means setting aside our own personal agendas in order to obey Him with our whole hearts. We demonstrate our humble devotion, our respect and the inestimable value we place upon Him by doing what He says. As Jesus Himself declared, when we love Him we will seek to obey Him fully (John 14:15).

3. Giving God Thanks

Thanksgiving flows from a recognition that all our benefits come from *God's* goodness and commitment to *us*, not from *our* goodness or commitment to *Him*. We haven't motivated God to love us: It is He who has motivated us to love Him.

Discerning believers recognize God as the source of their blessing — not their own dedication and discernment. Thanksgiving will be established in our hearts as we progressively realize that all the benefits we enjoy in time and in eternity come from Him, not from us.

Seeing who He is and what He endured and accomplished for us on the cross inspires our thanksgiving to Him. Christ Jesus paid the price.

4. Giving God Worship

For too long we have had the image of a distant God who is good to us only occasionally. But as we recognize His sovereignty, majesty, divine excellencies and perfections, we will be utterly captured by the beauty and splendor of His personality. As we see God's incomparable worth in relationship to everything else, our hearts will erupt and overflow in worship.

5. Casting Our Crowns Before the Lord

The climactic response of the twenty-four elders' worship was to take off their golden crowns and, without hesitation, cast them before God's throne. I believe the crowns in heaven symbolize the believers' eternal reward as a result of their personal achievements through the grace of God.

When you and I stand before the judgment seat of Christ, and our earthly lives and works are evaluated, all that was initiated and sustained by man, all that was impure, valueless and earthly — the wood, hay and stubble — will be burned up (1 Cor. 3:11-15). Only that which was born out of pure motives is of eternal value. Gold, silver and precious stones, representing all that was Spirit-initiated and Spirit-sustained in our lives, will endure the fire and pass through unscathed. Any treasures, any crowns we receive in heaven represent all we are and all we have attained as we cooperated with the gracious work of the Holy Spirit in our lives. The crowns were forged in the costly, sometimes painful, fires of obedience, and they are ours forever. But we will have no desire to keep them for ourselves. Without hesitation, in extravagant abandonment, we will cast them at the Lord's feet.

We must never allow our attainments to become our idols. As Paul reminded the Corinthians, "What do you have that you did not receive? But if you did receive it, why do you boast as if you had not received it?" (1 Cor. 4:7). Without God, we would be nothing and we could accomplish nothing.

My two young sons, Luke and Paul, provided me with an "illustrated sermon" along this line. When Luke was about six and Paul was around four years of age, they came to me and said, "Dad, we don't have any money, and your birthday is coming up." So I thumbed through my wallet and handed them a five-dollar bill. (Then I thought it over and gave them twenty dollars, instead!)

My sons took the money I gave them and went out to buy me a present. They came back and presented me with a brightly wrapped package, innocently assuming it was all a total surprise to me. Those two little guys were so excited. They could hardly wait for me to tear off the bow and paper and open the box.

As I pulled out the beautiful shirt they had chosen, exclaiming how much I liked it, I saw such pride and joy sparkling in their eyes. "We bought it for you, Dad!" they chorused. "Can you believe it?" Even though I had given them the money to buy the present, as I looked into their gleaming eyes, my heart, like theirs, was flooded with tremendous joy and satisfaction. It was such a wonderful, warm exchange.

That's the way it will be when we stand before our heavenly Father. It won't be "our" ministries or "our" successes and attainments that earned us the crowns we will cast in extravagant abandonment at His feet. Those crowns won't have one thing to do with "our" mailing lists or "our" prominence. Without our God, we could have done nothing. Yet our Father's heart, like ours, will be swelling with delight when we take off our crowns and present them to Him.

Beholding the Throne

Does your mind wander aimlessly in prayer? Do you lack focus when you seek to commune with Jesus? I know what that's like. Sometimes my prayer times seem uninspired, too. But over the course of the years, our lives will be immeasurably enriched as we keep that appointment with God.

THIRTEEN

Beholding the
Glory Dimly

Back then, in my college days, I was trying so hard to find the secret to a successful prayer life, but it was absolutely eluding me. Although I read a lot of heavy books on prayer, the deeper life and communion with God, when it got down to actually praying, I was an absolute failure. Oh, I had carefully scheduled time to spend alone with God and was faithful to keep my appointments with Him most of the time. Yet my efforts at praying were frustrating and unfulfilling.

After months of drudgery and failure at praying, witnessing and fasting, I told God, "Lord, I really love You, but I don't like praying. I don't like witnessing. I absolutely hate fasting. And I don't like Bible study either, even though it's easier for me than praying or fasting. Other than that, I really love You, Lord. But I know I'm not doing very well."

I remember the awful condemnation and confusion I felt because I was striking out on the four "biggies" in devotional disciplines. However, I did enjoy attending Bible study meetings. I loved to sing the beautiful praise and worship songs. And I could overdose when it came to listening to good Bible teaching on tape. But I still remember the defeat I felt as I shook my head and sighed, "Lord...will I *ever* like talking to You?"

I was living with three other Christian guys in a college apartment. We all worked together in a campus ministry. Every night around 8:45, my roommates would see me start getting uptight because I was dreading my prayer time from nine to ten o'clock. I hated going into my room to pray. I knew the next hour was going to be horrible, lifeless and boring. But each evening at nine o'clock, there I'd be on my knees. By 9:02 I'd be praying something like this:

"Lord, thank You for arms and legs. Thank You for food to eat. Some people in poor countries don't have much to eat — help them, Jesus. Thank You for my mom and for Pat. Thank You for my five wonderful sisters. Thank You for uhhhh...oh, yeah...thanks for letting me be on the college football team. Help me play better. Help us win. Uhhhh...oh, man, fifty-three more minutes to go! OK, let me see...hmmm...thank You for America." Thataway, Mike! That's a good one! (I had to keep encouraging and talking to myself to stay with it.)

Sometimes I could hear a couple of my friends in the other room laughing at my dreadful routine. Every once in a while, they'd poke their heads in and say, "Man, why don't you just relax?" And I'd take a deep breath, square my shoulders as if I were about to tackle some giant and mutter, "I'm gonna do this thing if it kills me!"

But I was doing it all wrong. I'd completely misunderstood the whole purpose of devotional prayer. Consequently, I dreaded prayer time. But I'd made a vow to God that I'd pray an hour every night, and I made up my mind to stick with it, regardless.

As in a Mirror

One evening I was in the prayer room, and, as usual, I'd completely run out of things to say. I opened my Bible, searching for inspiration. As I read, it was as if a light came on inside of me.

> But we all, with unveiled face beholding *as in a mirror* the glory of the Lord, are being transformed into the same image from glory to glory, just as from the Lord, the Spirit (2 Cor. 3:18, italics added).

My mind suddenly took off. Hmmm...as in a *mirror*...I am beholding the glory of God as in a mirror. What's a mirror? Well, a mirror gives a perfect reflection. Wait a minute. A mirror much as we have *today* gives a perfect reflection. But two thousand years ago when Paul was writing, the mirrors of that day didn't even come close to giving a perfect reflection: "For now we see in a mirror dimly..." (1 Cor. 13:12).

Dimly! An ancient mirror made of polished metal would give a faint, inadequate, very dim reflection. It was as if the Lord said, "Beholding Me dimly is all I ever asked of you."

The idea that even dim beholdings are sufficient to transform a believer's life was totally new to me. Could it also be that uninspired prayer was sufficient fulfillment of God's condition for inward transformation? I'd thought all those agonizing hours I'd spent in the prayer room were wasted and meaningless because they hadn't felt inspired, energized and filled with divine vigor and life. I'd thought the only prayer time that would lead to my inward transformation was that in which I was moved to tears by the presence of God.

I suddenly remembered all those seemingly uninspired, unanointed, Oh-God-where-are-You? prayers. I could imagine the Lord saying, "Yes, those were dim, all right. But that time with Me was still transforming, because all I have ever asked is that you behold Me dimly."

A dim beholding...as in a mirror, dimly.... "Well, I can do that," I said to the Lord. "I can behold You dimly. Yes, sir, I'm an *expert* at beholding You dimly! That's been my problem."

The truth was dawning on me. Even seemingly unanointed, uninspired praying is significant to God! "This is fantastic!" I shouted. "I can do this! It's a progressive process. If I continue to pray — even those dim, difficult prayer times I'm so accustomed to will actually be changed one of these days. I'm slowly being transformed from glory to glory!"

I ran out of the prayer room and made the announcement to my startled roommates. "Guess what, you guys? Unanointed prayer is relevant!"

"What?"

"Unanointed prayer is relevant! It works! It doesn't matter if it's anointed. It doesn't matter if it's inspired. An uninspired, dim devotional life is relevant to God!"

That became my main message everywhere I went. Some of my friends on campus just shrugged and said, "Bickle is off on some weird kick about unanointed prayer!"

I don't think they ever really understood what I was trying to say. Maybe I didn't explain it very well. But that was all right. My heart had grasped God's liberating word of hope to me. I knew if I persevered in prayer — even dim prayer — there was absolutely no doubt about it: I would gradually be transformed!

An Unveiled Face

As I've continued to seek the Lord, I've discovered at least two key elements to the phrase "But we all, with unveiled face beholding as in a mirror" (2 Cor. 3:18). In Old Testament times, veiling the face was a way of signifying the great gulf between a person and God, and the need for a mediator. But God has invited us to come boldly — fearlessly, confidently, courageously — to His throne of grace (Heb. 4:16). We can stand before God in total security and confidence, knowing His heart is utterly ravished for us. We can come boldly, without a sense of failure, condemnation or accusation. Christ purchased us, and His gift of righteousness has made us clean and secure in God's presence.

The first element in coming to God with an unveiled face refers to coming with a boldness and confidence rooted in understanding the finished work of the cross. We accept no condemnation because Jesus took our place in God's judgment.

A second element to this phrase "with unveiled face" refers to honesty of heart. No deception. No phony façades and religious jargon. No cover-ups or excuses. We can open our hearts to the Lord and speak plainly of our failures, hurts, disappointments, fears and frustrations.

When one of my sons has blown it and is trying to give me a carefully rationalized excuse, I can imagine the Lord saying to me, "Like father, like son. That's how you sometimes talk to Me." Yet God feels even more love, tenderness and compassion toward us than we feel toward our own children.

We behold the glory of the Lord, setting our minds on the presence and person of Jesus Christ with *unveiled faces*. Every dim beholding of His glory is like a tiny step in the grace of God. If you and I are faithful in taking those little steps, we will gradually experience inward transformation. We will increasingly experience those trembling, rejoicing and kissing aspects of God's great grace described in Psalm 2:11: "Serve the Lord with fear, and rejoice with trembling."

We will be transformed into Christ's very own image in ever-increasing splendor and from one degree of glory to another. Dim beholding is fruitful beholding. It's a *beginning*.

From Glory to Glory

Most of us do not discern that the glory of God is present in us. So many times I have overlooked the great thing that God was doing in and through me. I can really identify with a discouraged fellow by the name of Zerubbabel. His story is told in the book of Zechariah.

After seventy years of captivity in Babylon, the Jews were finally allowed to return to their own land in Israel. Zerubbabel was appointed as governor of the new colony. Zechariah, a young prophet of priestly lineage, stood at Zerubbabel's side to encourage him in leadership.

When the people reached Jerusalem, they first set up the altar of burnt offerings. Then they proceeded to lay the foundation of the new temple amid the massive ruins. From here, let me give you the Mike Bickle paraphrase of Zechariah 4:6-10.

> Zerubbabel had tried to get people to work on rebuilding the temple, but they were so discouraged that nobody wanted to work. So the disheartened governor sat down on a huge stone, looking around at the heaps of rubble from what had been a great temple before the Babylonian army destroyed it.
>
> "Boy, this place is a mess," Zerubbabel sighed. "Why did we ever want to come back here anyway? There's nothing left of this city worth returning to. Toppled stones and debris everywhere. This place is a disaster."
>
> Just then, young Zechariah, the prophet, tapped Zerubbabel on the shoulder. "Hello," he said cheerily. "How's it going?"
>
> "What a disaster!" moaned Zerubbabel. "Nobody showed up for work again today. Here I am, 'the great restorer of the land of Israel.' I'm supposed to

raise up this temple to the glory of God, but I can't get anybody inspired to work on it."

"Zerubbabel, God is with you."

Looking up, Zerubbabel questioned, "God is *with us?*"

"Of course He is. The very fact that you're no longer in captivity but are in this land is evidence of God's grace. You're a lot closer to seeing this place restored than you think you are. God says that your hands have laid the foundation of this house, and your hands will finish it. But there's something you have to do first."

Zerubbabel moaned and shook his head.

"No, no. Listen to me. You can do it. See that stone over there almost hidden by grass and weeds? That's the capstone, the finishing stone for the new temple. It's the final stone the people will put into place, the stone that signifies the building is completed."

"Yeah, OK. So?"

"Well, God says you're to shout, 'Grace, grace!' to it."

"To what?"

"To the stone."

"I'm supposed to shout at a stone?"

"Listen to me, Zerubbabel. God said to tell you, 'It is not by might, nor by power, but by My Spirit.' You're supposed to put your confidence in the grace of God. That's what shouting 'Grace!' is all about. Come on now. Get up, walk over there and shout, 'Grace! Grace!' "

"Zechariah, I know you mean well. But I'm already having trouble getting people to follow me. If they see me standing out here in the middle of these weeds, shouting at a rock — "

"Zerubbabel, are you going to obey the Lord or

not? Are you going to trust His grace, or aren't you? Now say it!"

"OK. What have I got to lose? I'll do it. Here goes: Grace.... Grace....

"No, no, that will never do. You're supposed to *shout* it: Grace! Grace!

Zerubbabel's effort was something less than enthusiastic. After a couple of halfhearted shouts, both stood silently looking at the stone. Finally Zechariah said, "You know what's the matter with you, Zerubbabel? You're despising the day of small beginnings."

Zerubbabel made no reply. Zechariah continued, "Because you're not seeing a lot happening around you right now, you're counting these days as unimportant. You've thrown them away as irrelevant. But the very fact that you're here in the land is the beginning of the move of God. There is something very great He wants to perform."

"It doesn't feel like the move of God to me."

"That's because you're out of touch with how God sees it. You're despising what's happening now because it looks small. It is small, but it's real; it's legitimate. All these obstacles that look like a great mountain to you are going to become a flattened plain. You'll see the day when this temple is complete and the capstone is set in place. Why wait until that great, climactic day when the last finishing touch is put on the temple before you begin to see the validity of your work? Begin praising God right now, and trust Him that your efforts are relevant even in this day of small beginnings."

What happened to Zerubbabel when he was rebuilding the temple happens to many believers in the building of their own spiritual lives. They make the mistake of thinking they're wasting their time because they don't see or feel a lot happening when they begin seeking God and meditating on His Word.

But being transformed from glory to glory is an operation of the Holy Spirit on the inside — in our minds, wills and emotions. It is being strengthened with power through His Spirit in the inner man (Eph. 3:16).

There's a false notion among many Christians that the Word of God works only if you have ten hours a day to be shut up in a room all alone reading it. But the Word of God was written primarily to the 99 percent of the human race who will never be in "full-time," salaried positions of ministry.

God's promises aren't just for paid preachers. They're also for the everyday person on the street; the stressed-out mother dealing with a toddler stuck in the "terrible twos"; the truck driver; the clerk at Wal-Mart; the secretary; the stressed-out businessman; the schoolteacher and the courtroom lawyer. God's Word is for the believer who fell into sin and lost everything except a heart that still cries out for God.

Every Christian — any Christian — can be progressively transformed from glory to glory. The problem is our idea of glory. We have this idea that it's not glorious unless we experience the full, unmeasured, blinding glory of God radiating from His throne in heaven. Some people can't discern the reality of the presence of the glory of God.

The glory of God is not limited to a burning-bush encounter with God. It's not, as some people mistakenly think, either the full glory or no glory at all. Being transformed from glory to glory is a promise made to every believer. We can experience an ever-increasing measure of that glory in the small, subtle dimensions that often go unnoticed.

Suppose you are a new Christian. The fact that you think differently now from the way you did before you were saved is the beginning of the glory of God at work in your life. Before your conversion you may have rarely thought about what pleased God. But now you're experiencing a deep interest and concern in the things that delight Him. That's the beginning of the glory of God in your life. It's not a small thing. It may be only a beginning, but it counts!

Some believers have taken the next step. They're hungering to grow in their prayer lives. They're longing to be able to understand and be fed from the Scriptures. They're trying to minister Jesus to their mates and their children, or to people at work. Although they fail, the sheer presence of those desires is a manifestation of God's glory in their lives. That's the influence and work of the Holy Spirit. Don't despise those small beginnings.

As Christians, we are always planning ways to get free from sin. We certainly aren't dreaming up ways to cover sin and get away with it. But we go around with our heads down, feeling condemned because we aren't perfect yet. The fact that we are susceptible to condemnation reveals our deep caring and longing to please God. We must be taught not to minimize the value of our desires for obedience. Those desires are a manifestation of the ever-increasing glory of God in our lives.

The point I'm making is this: Some people's definition of the glory of God is so out of reach that they think they will never experience it. Consequently, these believers come to the conclusion that God is not real or that salvation doesn't really work. Yet all the time it's working a lot better than we have the discernment to comprehend. The rubble of the past is being cleared away. Slowly but surely, a foundation in God is being laid. Some day a beautiful temple will rise from the ruins. Begin shouting "Grace! Grace!" right now. Have confidence that "He who began a good work in you will perfect it" (Phil. 1:6).

Don't underestimate the grace of God. Don't despise the day of small beginnings. Don't say, "I'll never be any different. I'm always going to be in bondage to lust, anger and covetousness. I'll never be free." The glory of God is already at work in your life. Thank Him for the sincere desire you have to break free from sinful habits and walk in the Spirit. Those small beginnings are firm steps in the direction of full maturity.

Changed and Still Changing

Change is a difficult process. Throughout the history of the church, people have tried to reduce the process of transformation to a mechanical set of spiritual aerobics. Roman Catholics and evangelical denominations have their own versions of this sanctification machinery.

Here's the good news. Sanctification and transformation come from *beholding* — not from *striving!* I jumped through every religious hoop I could find, but it wasn't until I began to *behold* that my heart was transformed.

Paul was zealous beyond all his contemporaries, but he counted it all as dung (Gal. 1:14; Phil. 3:4-8). But when he beheld the resurrected Christ, he was transformed forever. As a Catholic, Martin Luther exhausted himself trying to perform all the exercises prescribed for holiness. But one day he had a revelation of God's grace, and both he and the church have never been the same since.

It seems that the Christian world has dived headlong into a never-ending cycle of recovery, self-help and how-to-do-it sermons, books and tapes. Most of the material is helpful but we must not forget this one important point: Transformation does not come from striving, nor from psychological techniques alone. Transformation comes from beholding the wonders of God and being consumed with the true knowledge of Christ. That fiery passion burns away many of the lingering problems from the past and puts present difficulties in perspective.

Many people make solemn resolutions about what they are going to do from now on or about what they are never going to do again. But unless God changes you, you'll always be the way you are. We may drag ourselves into the prayer closet on a regular basis, but only God can change the heart. It happens by His grace working in you. Grace is God's power enabling you to do and be more than you ever could in your own strength. Paul referred to God's grace as the source of all his accomplishments:

> But by the grace of God I am what I am, and His grace toward me did not prove vain; but I labored even more than all of them, yet not I, but the grace of God with me (1 Cor. 15:10).

Two decades have passed since that night in my room when "the light came on" for me in regard to consistent devotional prayer that lacks feelings of inspiration. Over the years, I've stuck with my schedule, adding more time with the Lord as my hunger for intimacy with Him has increased. For me, regular prayer time, Bible reading and fasting are not exercises to earn God's favor. The merit badge mentality is gone, and my relationship with God is no longer performance-oriented. The transforming power of my devotional life is in the beholding, even if I only behold dimly.

I actually enjoy prayer now, and it's *good*. I can even handle the unanointed times. I absolutely love reading, meditating and studying the Word. Witnessing is a joy. I've even come to appreciate how fasting can sharpen my focus on the Lord and eternal things.

So many things have changed for the good inside me. I now enjoy the spiritual disciplines I used to despise. Over the years I've discovered a stronger resistance in my heart toward some of the senseless, sinful things I once loved. I still find some things in my emotions and thinking that I don't like. I believe the Holy Spirit will strengthen and transform my inner man in those areas as well.

It's as if I gain victory over certain sinful areas that are evident when the Spirit's "microscope" is set to a magnification power of ten. But when the power of magnification is adjusted to one hundred, I see new depths of my carnality as I grow in the Spirit. But I'm not discouraged. As I continue in my fellowship with Jesus, beholding Him through the Word and in prayer, the process of transformation will continue. I'm confident that Christ will continually be more fully formed in me (Gal. 4:19).

So remember: Despise not the day of small beginnings. Start honoring God for every transforming step, no matter how small or insignificant it seems. And don't let uninspired prayer get you down or make you stop seeking the Lord. A "dim beholding" is all God has required of us. Dim beholdings are fruitful beholdings. Those dim beholdings, in time will be sufficient to transform us from glory to glory!

FOURTEEN

Wasting Your Life
on Jesus

To the southwest of Jerusalem lies a deep, narrow ravine with steep, rocky sides, known as the Valley of Hinnom, or "Gehenna." On the southern brow overlooking the valley, King Solomon built an altar to the god Molech who was honored through the fiendish custom of sacrificing infants to the fire gods. In this valley Ahaz and Manasseh, kings of Judah, sacrificed their sons as sacrifices, making them "pass through fire." The horrible practice seems to have been kept up for a considerable period of time.

King Josiah attempted to put an end to these abominations by polluting the idol altars, rendering them ceremonially unclean. From that time, Gehenna appears to have become the common cesspool of Jerusalem. The city emptied its sewage into the valley to be carried off by the waters of the brook Kidron. Fires were kept burning in the valley to consume the solid waste deposited there. The valley was filled with an overpowering stench and served as a receptacle of waste, refuse and all that defiled the holy city. It became symbolic of the place of waste, destruction and everlasting punishment. Jewish apocalyptic writers began to call the valley the entrance to hell. Later its name Gehenna became synonymous with hell itself.

The word *Gehenna*, occurring twelve times in the New Testament, is always translated "hell." It is the name for the eternal abode and place of final punishment for Satan, his evil forces and the wicked. Jesus Himself often used the term in reference to the destiny of the lost and as an awesome warning of the consequences of sin.

In view of those facts, I often consider Christ's words in John 3:16 in a little different light from the usual. Most of us can quote that familiar verse by heart: "For God so loved the world, that He gave His only begotten Son, that whoever believes in Him should not perish, but have eternal life." When we say "should not perish," we automatically think of eternal destruction in hell. Yes, it's true that Jesus proclaimed a message that could deliver mankind from perishing in that fiery trash heap called "hell," where all that would defile God's holy city — the New Jerusalem — are cast. But Jesus' words "should not perish" also mean that He wants to keep us from another kind of perishing — from wasting and throwing our lives away now, here on earth.

Many believers are leading futile, meaningless, frustrating lives. Oh, they're going to heaven, all right. But, in the meantime, they're literally wasting God's gift, throwing away the precious hour God has granted them on earth.

God created mankind with tremendous capacities and abilities. Speaking of man, it says in Hebrews: "Thou hast crowned him with glory and honor, and hast appointed him over the works of Thy hands; Thou hast put all things in subjection under his feet" (Heb. 2:7-8). God intends marvelous things for the redeemed. He desires that we be transformed into the image of His Son and that we make an impact for Him on the lives of others during our brief stay on the earth.

Your life won't be wasted in eternity. But that doesn't stop Satan from trying to get you to waste the life you're living now on earth. He wants you to fail and fall short of your potential in God. Jesus never intended believers to perish in any dimension of the word — in this life or in the one to come. If Jesus said whoever *believes* in Him should not perish, why then do we see so many Christians perishing in this life by squandering their earthly time and talents?

We must understand that the word *believe* means much more than a one-time reach to God in a desperate moment. The word *believe* implies a continual process of reaching out to God in faith and obedience, not only to avoid eternal destruction in hell, but also to avoid wasting our lives on earth by experiencing God's purpose now.

I want to do the extravagant thing for God. Out of love and gratitude I want to do that which is not required. I want Him to reap His full inheritance from my life. How tragic, how grievous, how totally unnecessary to be wasted in this age through carelessness, passivity and desire for other things.

You and I must be watchful. We must stay spiritually wide awake. We must not lose our focus or become trapped in wrong relationships. The kingdom of God is worthy of our watchfulness. We must not cultivate any desires that would hinder or quench our spiritual lives, lest on that day we suffer loss, and our lives be judged unfruitful and wasted.

Misunderstood Extravagance

It's a strange thing, but when we seek with all our hearts to do the will of God and obey Him fully, our families, friends, even people in places of spiritual authority (the very people who should know better) often misjudge and criticize us. For example, the religious leaders of His day ridiculed and opposed Jesus, and His own brothers and sisters sometimes misjudged Him. If those things happened to Christ, those who obey Him fully may expect to be misjudged as well.

We expect the world's value system to be way off-center, putting power, money and prestige above everything else. But the value system of the church is off-center, as well. For example, many Christians consider it unfortunate when a young believer with a bright mind or financial success chooses to bypass certain privileges and promotions in order to live his or her time and life in God more fully.

Many Christians sniff in disdain at "hyperspiritual, holier-than-thou fanatics" who make good salaries but choose to live simply, pouring their resources into the kingdom of God instead of spending it on lavish lifestyles for themselves. Some believers criticize and look down on Christian mothers who choose to stay at home and invest their lives in their children instead of in careers, clubs and clothes. Examples of the worldly value system that has invaded the church are all around us.

I remember the disappointment I saw registered on many faces when I made the decision not to pursue medical school and, instead, go into the ministry. After all, becoming a medical doctor had been my goal for years, and I'd worked hard at it. "But, Mike," people protested, "God has blessed you with a good mind, and you've always made good grades. You've already been assured by the medical school board that your acceptance into medical school is a sure thing. You can work for God as a doctor, too. You would still be helping people, and with a doctor's income, you could give a lot of money to the church and help the needy. Oh, Mike! You — a preacher? What a *waste!*"

God didn't call you or me to be "successful"; He called us to be *faithful.* If God calls you to become a medical doctor, you'd better do it because that's where you will be able to fulfill His highest purposes for your life. If God gifts you to be a mechanic, an attorney, a truck driver or a teacher, then you will never be fully fruitful doing something else. God doesn't measure success by sacrifice, salary or university degrees; He measures it by obedience and faithfulness. The world, and even some in the church, may look at you, shake their heads and sigh, "What a waste!" But in the end you will enjoy God's smile, His fruitfulness and His reward.

Why This Waste?

A woman whom I consider to have been one of the greatest saints in the New Testament was condemned for being "wasteful." The devotion she displayed for Jesus has strengthened my own resolve many times. I love her faith, courage and sensitivity to the things of God. I look forward to meeting Mary of Bethany in the eternal city some day.

The facts we have regarding Mary are few. She was the sister of Lazarus and Martha. She lived in Bethany about a mile east of the Mount of Olives in her sister Martha's house. She and her sister first appear in the tenth chapter of Luke, where Jesus commends Mary, who sat listening eagerly for every word that fell from His lips. She had "chosen the good part," "the one thing needful," while "Martha, cumbered about with much serving," was distracted by all her preparations.

The next mention of Mary is at the death and resurrection of her brother, Lazarus. After that we see Mary once more in Scripture. About a year had passed since the time Jesus had been a guest in Martha's home and she had complained,

"Lord, do You not care that my sister has left me to do all the serving alone? Then tell her to help me" (Luke 10:40). Now, just days before His crucifixion, Jesus had returned to Bethany.

On this occasion, Jesus was a guest in the house of Simon the leper. Matthew tells us that Mary, Martha and Lazarus were present. John adds: "They made Him a supper there, and Martha was serving" (12:1-2). I believe that in Martha and Mary we have represented the two types of people in the body of Christ. Both are valid. Both are diligent. Both are loved by Jesus Christ. Both can get out of balance. One is the service-oriented believer, and the other is the communion-oriented believer. The body of Christ would not function well without either one.

John 12:1-9 and Mark 14:3-9 describe what took place in Bethany at the home of Simon the leper. Jesus, Lazarus and the others were reclining at the table, and Martha was serving. That very day Jesus had told His disciples that after two days, the Passover would be coming, and He would be delivered up for crucifixion (Matt. 26:2), yet His words seem to have fallen on deaf ears. Everyone was sitting around eating, drinking and chatting merrily. Hadn't anyone heard what Jesus had said? Hadn't anyone understood?

From what happened next, it appears that one had. Without warning, Mary appeared, clutching an alabaster vial containing a costly perfume — a pound of pure nard worth three hundred denarii, a year's wages. Before anyone could stop her, Mary, following a Jewish custom where wealthy people anointed the bodies of their loved ones with costly oil before burial, broke the vial and began pouring its precious contents over Christ's head and anointing His feet. The next moment she was on her knees before Him, wiping His feet with her hair as the perfume's fragrance filled the entire house.

For an instant everyone in the room sat dumbstruck. Then their stunned silence was shattered by the angry objections of Judas Iscariot: "Why was this perfume not sold for three hundred denarii," he demanded, "and given to poor people?" John reveals the protesting disciple's true motives and intentions: "Now he said this, not because he was concerned about the poor, but because he was a thief, and as he had the money box, he used to pilfer what was put into it" (John 12:6).

Judas wasn't the only person criticizing Mary's extravagant display of devotion. Others present were also scolding her. Mark says they were "indignantly remarking to one another, 'Why has this perfume been wasted?' " (14:4,5).

That is often the reaction of people who "like" Jesus but do not deeply love Him. Anything above the minimum, anything of special value offered to Him — whether it be a remarkable musical talent, a brilliant mind or one's whole heart — is regarded as unnecessary wastefulness. Mary's devotion stands in sharp contrast to the shallow commitment of such followers of Christ.

When you begin to love Jesus as Mary of Bethany loved Him, sooner or later, you will receive scolding from others. Mark my words. Just because people have big names, big positions and big ministries doesn't always mean they have hearts full of affection.

Around that table in Simon's home, all the clamor quieted as Jesus began to speak. Surely He would reprimand Mary for her recklessness. After all, hadn't the Teacher taught about the prodigal son who wasted his substance with riotous living and about the steward who wasted his master's possessions? After feeding both the four thousand and the five thousand, hadn't Jesus instructed His disciples to gather up into large baskets all the leftover fragments of bread and fish that nothing might be wasted? Surely Mary was about to receive the sternest reprimand of her life!

Jesus' response stunned the group almost as much as Mary's actions had:

But Jesus said, "Let her alone; why do you bother her? She has done a good deed to Me. For the poor you always have with you, and whenever you wish, you can do them good; but you do not always have Me. She has done what she could; she has anointed My body beforehand for the burial. And truly I say to you, wherever the gospel is preached in the whole world, that also which this woman has done shall be spoken of in memory of her" (Mark 14:6-9).

"Let her alone, Thomas. Stop scolding her, Matthew. Philip, don't say another word to her. Judas, Peter, sit down. Mary's true heart has been revealed, just as your own are soon to be. I know exactly why she did what she did, and it was a good thing. This woman has done all she could do for Me."

Today, many Christians don't even recognize all the names of Christ's twelve apostles who were present and probably scolding her on that occasion. But we're still hearing sermons about Mary of Bethany and her act of devotion. Just as Jesus said, "...Wherever the gospel is preached in the whole world, that also which this woman has done shall be spoken of in memory of her" (Mark 14:9).

Both Mary and Martha ministered to Jesus that day. Going to great lengths to prepare a banquet worthy of the Master, Martha served her Lord a natural feast. Mary prepared Jesus a spiritual feast, something He could enjoy and feast on just two days before He endured the worst hours in His entire existence — from eternity past to eternity future. Mary gave Jesus something from her heart that He could carry with Him to the cross.

Giving Without Regard to Cost

There are no rules that say we all have to empty our bank accounts, close the doors of our businesses and take the next plane to Africa. Never make the mistake of thinking Jesus demands extravagance. He requires only the simple giving of our hearts in love and obedience, the taking up of our own crosses and following Him.

Some wealthy people can enjoy the luxury of extravagance — of living and giving without regard to cost. They may never have to look at a price tag. They can waste if they want to and never feel the effects financially. It makes no difference because they still have plenty left over. But this wasn't the case with Mary. She would probably feel the financial effects of her costly sacrifice for the rest of her life. Yet this woman broke her most precious earthly treasure and joyfully lavished it upon the most priceless Treasure of the ages who was about to be broken for her.

How do you suppose a young woman like Mary had acquired a bottle of perfume worth a year's wages? Nothing in these passages indicates that Martha, Mary or Lazarus was wealthy. But the fact that the house mentioned in the tenth chapter of Luke is referred to as Martha's house does imply several things. Either Martha was a widow and had inherited the house from her deceased husband; or the parents of Martha, Lazarus and Mary may have died, leaving the house to Martha since she was the eldest. (If Lazarus had been the eldest, by Jewish custom, the house would have gone to him.) It also makes us wonder if the costly perfume might have been left to Mary as part of the inheritance from their deceased parents. If so, the perfume must have represented Mary's financial security for her present and future. We have no way of knowing these things for sure, but some things are certain: The perfume belonged to Mary, and it was very expensive.

I'm sure that concerned friends and relatives later approached Mary asking, "What about tomorrow, Mary? You have no security now."

I can imagine her replying, "I have Him, and that's good enough for me. My future is in His hands. Over a year ago

Jesus told me I had chosen the good part which would not be taken away from me, and I'm putting my trust in what He said" (Luke 10:42).

Friendship With Jesus

One day as I sat meditating on what the Scriptures tell us about Mary of Bethany, I realized that on each of the three occasions where this young woman appears in the New Testament, she winds up at the feet of Jesus (see Luke 10:39, John 11:2, John 12:3). Based on the depth of devotion for Jesus we see in Mary's life, is it any wonder that Jesus loved Mary, Martha and Lazarus and cherished their special affection and friendship?

Bethany was only a mile or so, a twenty-minute walk, from Jerusalem. Six days before the Passover, Jesus made that walk to Bethany, to the home of Mary, Martha and Lazarus.

Why did He choose to spend the last six days of His life on earth with them? Why not with Nicodemus, a leading Pharisee, "a ruler of the Jews" and a member of the Sanhedrin, the spiritual and political senate of Israel? Jesus could have used that time to pour His strategies and purposes into this influential man, building him up spiritually, enabling him to stand firm in his strategic position during the trying days ahead.

Why didn't Jesus stay with Silas or with Barnabas, leaders in the early church from its beginning, men who lived in Jerusalem and who would later travel and minister with the apostle Paul? Why didn't He stay in the home of Joseph of Arimathea, a wealthy disciple who could have financed many things for the Jerusalem church, or with Matthias, who would later be chosen to occupy the ministry and apostleship vacated by Judas Iscariot? Why didn't Jesus go to the place where His own mother was staying?

Out of the 500 followers to whom He would appear after His resurrection and the 120 who would be present in the upper room on the day of Pentecost, why did Jesus choose to spend the remaining days of His life in the home of Martha, Mary and Lazarus? Perhaps one of the reasons was so that His disciples could serve as a protecting hedge about Lazarus, since the chief priests who were plotting Christ's death were scheming to put Lazarus to death, also (John 12:10). However, I'm inclined to believe His main reasons were that these three friends loved Him with great devotion and firmly believed He was the Christ — the Messiah. Their house was a sanctuary of peace, affection and rest. It was a place where He could relax, feel totally accepted and loved, and be strengthened for the grievous days ahead.

In this home, people were consumed with love for Jesus. Martha and Lazarus were loyal, devoted friends, and Mary was a person whose heart felt what His heart was feeling. Her attentive ears were able to catch the meaning of His veiled words. She was a friend who never partook in the disciple's arguments as to which of them was the greatest; who never tugged at Christ's sleeve, requesting the privilege of sitting at His right hand in the kingdom. She was simply Mary, His devoted friend. She realized what an inestimable privilege it was just to sit at His feet, bask in the beauty of His presence and drink in His every word.

Mary may have never been anointed to preach or to perform signs and wonders, but she was anointed with a weeping heart. The Scriptures never record that Mary of Bethany had a prominent ministry like some of the others. But during Christ's final days before Calvary, this woman's beautiful, worshipful spirit must have ministered greatly to the Son of God.

Wasting Our Lives on Jesus

Jesus Christ loves the world and He loves the church, but there's a special bread He feeds those who love Him in private. There's a divine manna He reserves for those who extravagantly waste themselves in His presence.

None of us has an option when it comes to whether or not

our lives will be wasted. The only option we have is *how* we will waste them. All of us will waste our lives either in sin and compromise, passivity and the cares of this life, or we will waste them on Jesus. We can waste our lives on serving the devil and end up in a flaming trash heap called hell, or we can waste our lives and our resources on Jesus as Mary did, laying up treasure in heaven where moths and rust won't corrupt it and thieves can't break through and steal it. O God, give us grace to live as Mary did.

How do you waste your life on Jesus? Easy. It's no secret. Make the decision in your mind, and your heart will catch up. Get in His presence. Reject sin. Cry out to Him in prayer. Lift your soul to Him in worship. Read and meditate on the Word until your heart is filled with the things that fill God's heart. Utterly abandon yourself to Him, for intimacy with God takes time, and there is no substitute for waiting in His presence. Like Mary, choose to forego some of the less important things going on around you in order to make more time to cultivate a relationship with Him. Lavishly, extravagantly pour out your life as a drink offering upon the holy altar of God. Allow yourself to be broken and spilled out for the priceless One whose body was broken and whose precious life's blood was spilled out for you.

Lord Jesus, in sweet abandon, let me be spilled out and used up for You!

Is that your prayer? Then rearrange your schedule to make time for Him.

Why don't you take my hand and come with me just for a moment? Stand here and gaze through the door John opened for us into that invisible world. It's the world you and I could be living in tomorrow — the world where we will be living ten billion years from now.

There! Do you see it? A rainbow-encircled throne! Seated upon the throne is the One who lives forever and ever. Amid the seven lamps of fire burning before the throne do you see those winged creatures that look so strange to our eyes? Can you hear them crying, "Holy, holy, holy"? Watch now! When the living creatures give glory, honor and thanks to Him who was and who is and who is to come, the twenty-four white-robed elders will prostrate themselves before the throne, worshipping God.

Do you see Him? The Lamb who purchased men for God with His own blood and made them to be a kingdom and priests to God. He is there. Look! Listen! Surrounding the throne, the living creatures, the elders and the Lamb are thousands and thousands of angels, and they are all crying, "To Him who sits on the throne, and to the Lamb, be blessing and honor and glory and dominion forever and ever" (Rev. 5:13). Do you hear them? Can you see that great cloud of witnesses, composed of believers of all the ages, assembling as one mighty nation?

Would you like to walk up before the throne and bow down? We can. We don't have to draw back in fear or shame. There beside the Father is Christ, our high priest. He understands our weaknesses and infirmities. He sympathizes with our liability to the assaults of temptation, for He has been tempted in every respect as we are, but without sinning.

There's no need to be timid. We're not trespassing on forbidden ground. We have actually been *invited* to come here. I've read the invitation myself, and it says we may *fearlessly, confidently, boldly draw near* to God's throne of grace that we may receive mercy for our failures and find grace to help us in our time of need (Heb. 4:14-16).

Since we've been invited, I come to the throne often to meditate, to gaze, to expose my spirit to the majesty and eternity and holiness of our glorious King and to put earthly things into eternal perspective. I bring my needs and cares, my confessions and commitments, my appeals and my attainments and present them to Him. I watch as they rise like sweet-smelling incense before the Lord.

Before we go, let's just kneel here for a moment together...before the throne.

Chapter 3

1. J. I. Packer, *Knowing God* (Downers Grove, Ill.: Inter-Varsity Press, 1973), p. 6.
2. A. W. Tozer, *The Knowledge of the Holy* (New York: HarperCollins Publishers, 1961), p. 76.
3. Ibid., p. 23.
4. Ibid., pp. 129, 131.

Chapter 4

1. William Wordsworth, "The world is too much with us," in *Sound and Sense*, Laurence Perrine and Thomas R. Arp (Orlando, Fla.: Harcourt Brace Jovanovich College Publishers, 1992), pp. 46-47.

Chapter 5

1. C. H. Spurgeon, *The Treasure of David: An Expository and Devotional Commentary on the Psalms*, vol. 1 (Grand Rapids, Mich.: Baker Book House, 1983), p. 11.
2. Ibid.

Chapter 6

1. A. W. Tozer, *The Knowledge of the Holy*, p. 6.
2. Merrill F. Unger, *Unger's Bible Dictionary* (Chicago: Moody Press, 1966), p. 378.
3. Tozer, *The Knowledge of the Holy*, p 6.

Chapter 10

1. Iain Murray, *Puritan Hope* (Carlisle, Pa.: Banner of Truth, 1979).

Chapter 11

1. J. I. Packer, *Knowing God*, p. 194.

Chapter 12

1. Tozer, *The Knowledge of the Holy*, p. 123.
2. Helen H. Lemmel, "Turn Your Eyes Upon Jesus," copyright © 1922 Singspiration Music Inc. All rights reserved. Used by permission of Benson Music Group, Inc.

We want you to have Mike Bickle's *Personal Prayer List*
FREE

You've probably just finished reading *Passion for Jesus* by Mike Bickle and may be wondering how you can get other resource materials by Mike. Well, we want to give you a gift by sending you a copy of his *Personal Prayer List*. Through this booklet he offers practical suggestions for turning Scripture to prayer and offering it back to the Lord as a powerful tool for advancing the kingdom. Mike's years of experience in the prayer closet make this a valuable tool for helping you develop your own devotional prayer life. Just write to us at the address below! We'll send you a copy of his *Personal Prayer List* along with a coupon good for 35% off your next tape order from our catalog of Mike's ministry resources. Quantities of this booklet are limited and will be filled on a first-come, first-served basis.

Detach here and mail

Name _____

Address _____

City _____ State_____ Zip _____

Name of Church You Attend _____

Church Address _____

City _____ State_____ Zip _____

❑ Please send information about Grace Training Center of Kansas City.
❑ Please send information about Metro Vineyard Conferences with Mike Bickle.
❑ Please send a resource catalog of Mike Bickle's ministry aids.
❑ I have high school- or college-age youth living in my home.

About Metro Vineyard's Master's Commission...

The Master's Commission is a nine-month resident discipleship training program for men and women between the ages of 18 and 24. It serves as a "boot camp" of intense Christian life training, combining solid biblical teaching, life-challenging curriculum and practical experience. This program is an opportunity for students to broaden the foundation of their lives by giving themselves to serving the body through a practical daily lifestyle and learning about the Lordship of Jesus. During this training time the student will experience many ministry opportunities with training concentrating on:

- Servanthood
- Character building
- Studying and applying the Bible

- Ministry of the Word
- Worship and intercession
- Evangelism and outreach

For information about Grace Training Center, please fill out the form on the reverse side and send it to us.

About Metro Vineyard Conferences...

Metro Vineyard Fellowship hosts conferences periodically in Kansas City for training, equipping and encouraging the body of Christ at large. Joining Mike Bickle and the Metro Vineyard Fellowship leadership team are leaders from around the nation. If you would like to receive information about future conferences hosted by Metro Vineyard Fellowship, please fill out the form on the reverse side and send it to us.

Place
Stamp
Here

GRACE MINISTRIES
P.O. Box 229
Grandview, MO 64040-229

GRACE TRAINING CENTER
A Biblical Foundation for a Lifetime of Passion, Purity and Power

Sam Storms, Ph.D.
PRESIDENT
"Our desire is to impart tomorrow's leaders with fresh power and a new vision through the life-changing knowledge of God."

Mike Bickle
DIRECTOR
"Grace Training Center combines serious academic study in the Word of God with practical ministry training. Our desire is that you leave GTC more in love with Jesus and better equipped to serve Him."

OTHER FACULTY

Wes Adams, M.A., M.Div., Ph.D.
Robb Black, M.A.
Jim Goll, B.S.
Lee Harms, M.S., Ph.D.
Michael Kailus, M.S., M.Div.
George LeBeau, Th.M.
Philip Pidgeon, D.Min.

Noel Alexander, M.Div.
Avner Boskey, Th.M.
Tim Gustafson, M.Div., S.T.M.
Fred Herron, M.Div., D.Min.(cand.)
Ron Lawlor, M.A.
Bruce McGregor, M.Div.

"I am happy to recommend Grace Training Center to people who are seeking deeper training for ministry but are unable to attend a theological seminary. I am confident that GTC will provide sound training in the Bible and theology, mature instruction in practical ministry skills and scripturally guided experience of ministry in the power of the Holy Spirit."

Wayne Grudem, Ph.D.
Trinity Evangelical Divinity School

"I heartily recommend the Grace Training Center to anyone hungry for more of God's Word and the skills to minister in the power of the Holy Spirit. Grace Training Center provides a unique opportunity for depth in biblical studies and growth in devotion to God."

Jack Deere, Th.D
Author, *Surprised By the Power of the Spirit*

TO SEND FOR MORE INFORMATION, FILL OUT THE FORM ON ADJOINING PAGE.

If you enjoyed *Passion for Jesus*, you'll love
these other new Creation House titles:

Hippo in the Garden
by James Ryle

Author James Ryle says that God speaks to us
at unusual times in unexpected places.
Through his humorous personal anecdotes
and references to the Old and New Testament Scriptures,
you will discover that every circumstance of life
becomes an opportunity to converse with God.

Keeping Your Dreams Alive
When They Steal Your Coat
by Doug Murren

Author Doug Murren will inspire you to see
your dreams to fulfillment — no matter what happens to you
along the way. With a dash of humor, Murren shows how
the life of Joseph is a practical model for today's dreamers.
You don't have God's dreams — they have you!

There's a Miracle in Your House!
by Tommy Barnett

God wants to do something fantastic
with what you already have!
This upbeat, motivating book will revolutionize
the way you think about "impossible" situations
and "overwhelming" opportunities.
When God shows you the miracle in the house,
you won't have to look anywhere else.

Available at your local Christian bookstore or from:

Creation House
600 Rinehart Road
Lake Mary, FL 32746
1-800-283-8494